T0312303

Cambridge Elements ≡

Elements in Ancient and Pre-modern Economies
edited by
Kenneth Hirth
Pennsylvania State University
Emily J. Kate
University of Vienna
Timothy Earle
Northwestern University

THE AZTEC ECONOMY

Frances F. Berdan
California State University, San Bernardino

CAMBRIDGE
UNIVERSITY PRESS

Shaftesbury Road, Cambridge CB2 8EA, United Kingdom

One Liberty Plaza, 20th Floor, New York, NY 10006, USA

477 Williamstown Road, Port Melbourne, VIC 3207, Australia

314–321, 3rd Floor, Plot 3, Splendor Forum, Jasola District Centre,
New Delhi – 110025, India

103 Penang Road, #05–06/07, Visioncrest Commercial, Singapore 238467

Cambridge University Press is part of Cambridge University Press & Assessment,
a department of the University of Cambridge.

We share the University's mission to contribute to society through the pursuit of
education, learning and research at the highest international levels of excellence.

www.cambridge.org
Information on this title: www.cambridge.org/9781009368094

DOI: 10.1017/9781009368124

First published 2023

A catalogue record for this publication is available from the British Library.

ISBN 978-1-009-36809-4 Paperback
ISSN 2754-2955 (online)
ISSN 2754-2947 (print)

The Aztec Economy

Elements in Ancient and Pre-modern Economies

DOI: 10.1017/9781009368124
First published online: March 2023

Frances F. Berdan
California State University, San Bernardino

Author for correspondence: Frances F. Berdan, fberdan@csusb.edu

Abstract: This Element provides a synthesis and updated examination of the Aztec economy (AD 1325–1521). It is organized around seven components that recur with other Elements in this series: historic and geographic background, domestic economy, institutional economy, specialization, forms of distribution and commercialization, economic development, and future directions. The Aztec world was complex, hierarchical, and multifaceted and in a constant state of demographic growth, recoveries from natural disasters, political alignments and realignments, and aggressive military engagements. The economy was likewise complex and dynamic and characterized by intensive agriculture, the exploitation of nonagricultural resources, utilitarian and luxury manufacturing, wide-scale specialization, merchants, markets, commodity monies, and tribute systems.

Keywords: Aztecs, ancient economies, ancient trade, land and labor, tribute

ISBNs: 9781009368094 (PB), 9781009368124 (OC)
ISSNs: 2754-2955 (online), 2754-2947 (print)

Contents

1 Space and Time in the Aztec World

Economic systems, the Aztec economy included, do not exist in vacuums. They consist of organizations and activities that operate "on the ground." They draw on known histories, traditions, and expectations. And they are intricately connected to social, political, and religious entities. In other words, to understand the Aztec economy we must establish this culture's background along three dimensions: historic, geographic, and social-political-religious.

Before we pursue these backdrops, it is necessary to clarify the use of some often ambiguous and confusing terms. "Aztec" is first and foremost. This term, which gained popularity beginning early in the nineteenth century, was not used by the people of central Mexico in pre-Spanish times. It is, however, part of the title of this Element and does have its place: It is used here to refer to the Nahuatl-speaking people of the Basin of Mexico during the Late Postclassic period (AD 1350–1521). "Aztec empire," also called the Triple Alliance empire, refers to the imperial entity built by the city-states of Tenochtitlan, Texcoco, and Tlacopan from AD 1430 to AD 1521. The term "Aztec" also designates specific chronological periods as well as imperial architectural and artistic styles.

But there is still a major pitfall: "Aztec" is often equated with "Mexica," or "Colhua-Mexica," the specific ethnic group that settled and lived in the twin island cities of Tenochtitlan and Tlatelolco. Since people were identified not only by ethnicity but also by city-state residence, the Mexica were also called (and called themselves) Tenochca or Tlatelolca. We therefore read about the Chalca of Chalco, the Xochimilca of Xochimilco, and so on – this was how they identified themselves, and others, on a day-to-day basis. Some also referenced their language: Nahuatl ("good speech"), Otomí, Tlalhuica, Totonaca, and so on. These more nuanced designations allow us to better see the people as they saw themselves. They also highlight the fragmented nature of this landscape: Individual city-states vied with one another for supremacy (often through warfare), and ethnic groups overtly expressed their unique qualities and differences from one another. The use of the term "Aztec" implies a cultural and political unity and uniformity that simply did not exist at the time. Although I use the term here as defined, when appropriate I prefer to use the identities that the people themselves used. Also found throughout this Element is "Mesoamerica," which refers to the culture area encompassing the areas of Mexico and Central America that saw the rise and fall of complex states and civilizations before the arrival of the Spaniards (Figure 1). Comparatively, Mesoamerica exhibits a certain economic uniqueness among the world's early civilizations: It combined the sole use of human porters and canoes for transport, a lack of large domesticated animals, and a system of highly developed markets.

Figure 1 Regions of Mesoamerica. Drawing by Jennifer Berdan Lozano.

1.1 Historic Background

This case is essentially confined to the years AD 1325–1521. The Mexica established their island city of Tenochtitlan in the year Two House or AD 1325, the year that serves as the benchmark for this presentation of the Aztec economy. However, significant economic foundations were laid long before that date, and the Aztecs drew heavily on that earlier-established economic base.

The long pre-Columbian history of Mesoamerica saw the rise and fall of several grand civilizations, including the Olmec of the Gulf Coast (ca. 1200 BC–300 BC), the Classic Maya of southern Mesoamerica (ca. AD 250–900), Teotihuacan in the northeastern Basin of Mexico (ca. AD 1–650), and the Toltecs of Tula, approximately seventy kilometers north of the Basin of Mexico (AD 950–1175). It must be kept in mind that these are only the most highly touted early civilizations; many other complex social and political entities developed throughout Mesoamerica during this time period. By the time these civilizations took root, agriculture was already well in hand; highly productive varieties of maize, beans, squashes, chilis, and other plants (for foods, fibers, and medicines) were developed. Agricultural techniques such as crop rotation, terracing, canal irrigation, hydraulic constructions, swampland reclamation, and raised fields (*chinampas*) were used in pre-Aztec civilizations, depending on their local situations. Additionally, these people were experienced in many procedures for resource extraction and techniques of manufacture such as stonework, spinning and weaving, pottery making, metallurgy, book making, and feather working. They applied their knowledge and skills to urban planning, monumental constructions such as temples and palaces, and massive works of art. They also moved goods over short and long distances, although our understanding of the exact nature of these movements and exchanges is still murky for the earliest civilizations. At least by the times of Teotihuacan and Tollan (Tula), the most relevant civilizations to the Aztecs themselves, specialized production, merchants, markets, and differential consumption patterns can all be seen in the archaeological record (Diehl, 2004; Hirth et al., 2020; Pool, 2012; Stark and Ossa, 2010; Wells, 2012).

As for the various Aztec peoples themselves, they first appear in the Mesoamerican historical saga as *chichimeca*, peoples usually described as nomadic or seminomadic hunters and gatherers who traveled south from the northern Mexican deserts, ultimately settling in highland regions of central Mexico. There were apparently fairly substantial waves of these populations, moving southward over centuries, often stopping here and there for periods of time. They were diverse in social affinities and ethnic identities and exhibited different degrees of societal complexity. The Mexica, as the last of these groups, practiced maize cultivation, built dams and *chinampas*, wore capes (albeit "tattered") rather than animal skins, constructed temples, had priests, worshipped multiple deities, and were familiar with fine luxuries such as cacao and precious greenstones. It is clear that "the Mexica and many other *chichimeca* were at least somewhat prepared for their transition from a nomadic to a settled lifestyle" (Berdan, 2021: 41; Anderson and Schroeder, 1997).

When they entered the Basin of Mexico, it was already crowded with city-states competing with one another for economic viability and political supremacy (Figure 2). Once settled on their unpromising island site of Tenochtitlan, the Mexica found a niche by successfully serving the powerful city-state of Azcapotzalco as mercenaries. In addition to gaining economic rewards, this service earned them a reputation as fierce warriors. Early on, the Mexica set about constructing a temple for their patron god Huitzilopochtli and began laying out and building their city by trading their lacustrine resources to lakeshore peoples for building materials. They also firmly established a royal dynasty, negotiated strategic elite marriages, and forged advantageous political alliances. Their population grew along with their wealth and reputation. By 1428, just over a century from Tenochtitlan's founding, the Mexica were recognized as a potentially powerful, competitive, and threatening city-state.

The other city-states in the Basin had rightful cause for worry, for in 1428–30 the Mexica allied with the Acolhua of Texcoco and the Tepaneca of Tlacopan to throw off their dependence on powerful Azcapotzalco. With little hesitation, the

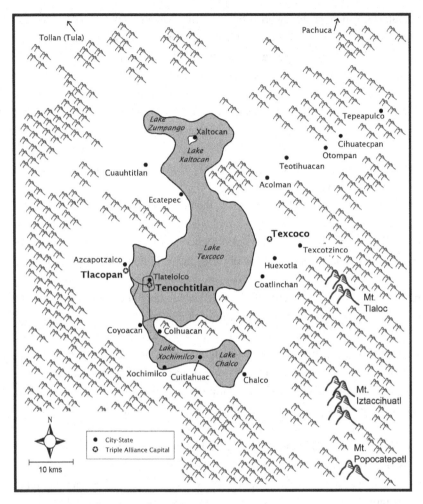

Figure 2 Basin of Mexico city-states. Drawing by Jennifer Berdan Lozano.

rulers of this Triple Alliance embarked on an aggressive agenda of political control through military conquests and cunning alliances. They began with conquests within the Basin itself, moving rapidly beyond that heartland in every direction to attain and consolidate economic and political control on an imperial scale. This involved diverse strategies of empire building through the reigns of six Mexica rulers. There were military conquests and demands of regular payments of tribute – this resulted in domains we customarily call "tribute provinces" that were usually still ruled by their local kings and only loosely controlled by the empire. But conquests were expensive at long distances; the Triple Alliance powers solved this problem by forging asymmetrical alliances along distant hostile borderlands and critical trade routes. These allied "client states" held those borderlands in check for the empire and protected major commercial networks throughout the imperial domain. We call these "strategic provinces" (Berdan et al., 1996). This may sound straightforward, but the imperial century was uneasy, unsettling, and somewhat unpredictable: Warfare was endemic, conquest motives were fabricated, enemies fomented rebellions, royal ambassadors were assassinated, powerful rulers intimidated, spies spied, and people were sometimes forced to leave their homes in response to military action or natural disasters such as droughts and floods. Enemies became allies, and then back again, almost overnight.

Imperial rulers also engaged some professional merchants (*pochteca* and *oztomeca*) as state agents and spies: They carried their king's goods beyond imperial boundaries to trade with distant rulers in international trading centers or spied on adversaries in distant marketplaces. As economic entrepreneurs, these merchants traveled far and wide to ferret out economic opportunities that might be exploited by the imperial powers. Additionally, strategic elite marriages continued to be effective in connecting allied and subject rulerships, and the overwhelming military might and expanding wealth of the Triple Alliance powers served to intimidate intractable enemies. But imperial strategies were not always successful and enemies persevered, the most powerful being the Tarascans to the west and Tlaxcalla and its allies to the east. The empire, as we see it in 1519 on the eve of the Spanish conquest, was powerful, wealthy, and intimidating, but at the same time it was loosely controlled and perhaps a bit too sprawling, with rebellions seemingly on the increase.

This was the empire encountered by the Spaniards who, along with their native allies, conquered the Mexica and dismantled the Aztec empire. Economically, the Spaniards introduced foods such as wheat, sugarcane, and grapes (for wine) and domesticated animals such as horses, cattle, mules, donkeys, pigs, sheep, goats, and chickens. They brought iron tools (machetes, knives, plows, and scissors, for example) and practical use of the wheel (for transport, spinning, and pottery production). They introduced distilling (for tequila), candle making, and stringed instruments, as well as large treadle looms for weaving. But many aspects of the pre-Spanish economy persisted: Women continued to weave on backstrap looms, people continued to drink *pulque* from maguey sap, European clothing merged with native garments, and cacao bean money circulated alongside Spanish coins in thriving Indigenous marketplaces.

1.2 Geographic and Cultural Landscapes

The Aztec domain lay entirely within the tropics. While this may suggest geographic uniformity, considerable variations in landscapes exist, largely shaped by rainfall patterns, altitude zones, and topography. Rainfall is seasonal, with the year divided into wet (May–October) and dry (November–April) seasons. This customary pattern is only a generalization – rains can begin late, appear during the winter months, or not come at all. Summer rainfall often falls in great torrents. Too little or too much rain was a perennial problem for the Aztecs who suffered epic droughts and floods.

A convenient way of comprehending the environmental diversity in Mesoamerica is the oft-used *tierra caliente, tierra templada*, and *tierra fria* altitudinal scheme. *Tierra caliente* (hot land) consists of hot, humid lands extending from sea level to an elevation of 1,000 meters (3,280 feet). It encompasses coastal lowlands (Gulf and Pacific) and inland hilly areas that exhibit high rainfall, lush tropical vegetation, diverse wildlife, and the potential for abundant and reliable crop yields. These lands were prized by the Aztecs as sources of cacao, cotton, precious stones, jaguar pelts, and exquisite feathers. *Tierra templada* (temperate land) rose above 1,000 meters to 2,000 meters (6,560 feet) in elevation. Local environments in this zone range from dry scrublands to rolling hills and sprawling grasslands to mountain forests. Rivers and deep barrancas provide definition and drama to these mountain-and-valley landscapes. The Aztec empire targeted this zone for staple foodstuffs and localized resources such as bees' honey, dyes and pigments, paper, gold, copper, and turquoise.

Tierra fria (cold land) lies above 2,000 meters: These are lands of broad highland plateaus, interior-drainage basins, and majestic volcanoes. In Aztec times, *tierra fria* supplied resources such as staple foodstuffs, maguey, timber, obsidian, reeds, clay for pottery, and salt on its abundant arable lands, pine-oak forests, and mountain-rimmed basins with large lakes. One of these, the Basin of Mexico, was the heartland of the Aztec empire. This Basin was dominated by five lakes that coalesced into a single body of water during the rainy season; the lakes themselves offered up an abundance of lacustrine and lakeshore resources, provided the setting for intensive agriculture (*chinampas*), and attracted millions of migratory birds annually. This all sounds quite attractive, but the people frequently faced disasters on a grand scale – droughts, frosts, floods, earthquakes, and vermin infestations interrupted and severely disrupted their daily lives.

By the early sixteenth century, the Mexica city of Tenochtitlan was home to an astounding 200,000–250,000 people, although most Basin cities ranged from around 2,000 to 25,000 people (Smith, 2008: 152). By comparison, Seville's population, for that time, is estimated at 55,000. The Basin itself (at about 7,000 square kilometers or 2,700 square miles) was home to approximately a million people. If we extend our view beyond the Basin to the larger imperial domain, we are talking about perhaps as many as 25 million people spread over approximately 200,000 square kilometers (77,220 square miles).

In the Basin and throughout the empire, in cities and in the countryside, people lived their everyday lives in households – some large, some small, some in-between. The largest of these, royal and noble palaces, contained many rooms, courtyards, and gardens and were exquisitely appointed – all to serve administrative functions and large polygynous families. Houses of commoners ranged from multiroom compounds to single-room dwellings, depending on the householders' status and wealth. Nuclear or extended families, along with other unrelated people, lived and worked in these households; they were the most fundamental social and economic units in Aztec society.

But that is only the beginning of the story. Households were grouped into residential neighborhoods called *calpolli* or *tlaxilacalli*; people were bound together in these neighborhoods through a common leader, patron deity, temple, and military school, along with shared labor, tribute, and ceremonial duties. *Calpolli* combined to form *altepetl*, or city-states, arguably the most important political units in Aztec times. As the basic building blocks of Aztec political life, *altepetl* exhibited "a legitimate ruling dynasty, a sense (if not the actuality) of political autonomy, control over local lands and labor, a well-established founding legend, often with mythological underpinnings, and a patron deity complete with temple" (Berdan, 2014: 135–136). Tribute was assessed and paid by *altepetl*. Some city-states became well-known for particular economic occupations, as exceptional marketplaces, or as pilgrimage destinations. *Altepetl* opportunistically warred and forged alliances with one another, creating a highly volatile political environment.

Spatially, city-states typically consisted of an urban center (capital city) and surrounding rural settlements and farmland. The capital city was the political, economic, and religious hub of the *altepetl*; it was the seat of the city-state's ruler (*tlatoani*, pl. *tlatoque*) and his palace, and it encompassed the major temples, ballcourt, marketplace(s), and other civic buildings. It was the scene of the most spectacular ceremonies held in the city-state. City-states also typically exhibited a predominant ethnicity, although, with many large and small movements and resettlements of people, most were multiethnic and multilingual.

Beyond residence and ethnicity, people were also distinguished by social class. This was an intensely hierarchical system. Rulers and other high-ranking nobles made political decisions, lived grandly, and had important social and economic responsibilities to their communities. Most of the population (perhaps 95 percent) were commoners: farmers, fishermen, porters, midwives, masons, artisans, merchants, and myriad others. They differed considerably in wealth and status, ranging from wealthy professional merchants to humble landless farmers. At the bottom of the social pyramid were slaves who were often attached to others in order to pay off gambling debts or stolen property.

In Aztec times, the Basin of Mexico was crowded with an estimated thirty to fifty *altepetl*. Three of these, Tenochtitlan, Texcoco, and Tlacopan, absorbed the others into their Triple Alliance empire. Beyond the Basin, this empire controlled about 450 city-states by 1519 (Smith, 2003). Household, *calpolli*, *altepetl*, and empire – these were the essential social and political entities within and through which the complex economies of the Aztec world operated.

1.3 Sources

Although flourishing more than 500 years in the past, Aztec economic life can be reconstructed through a variety of sources. The Aztec elite (perhaps exclusively) were literate and produced innumerable pictorial books (*codices*) housed in vast palace and temple libraries. Unfortunately, most of these are now lost, and for the Mexica themselves, perhaps only one codex produced in pre-Spanish times (*Matrícula de Tributos*) has survived. Still, now-lost pictorials sometimes served as the bases of Indigenous and Spanish narratives, and many were composed in the early colonial period by native scribes presenting native content (such as maps, genealogies, histories, and tribute tallies) in native styles. Among the most significant of these are the *Codex Mendoza*, which documents Aztec history, tribute accounts, and daily life (Berdan and Anawalt, 1992), and the *Florentine Codex* compendium, illustrated and written in Nahuatl by native scribes and supervised by the Franciscan friar Sahagún (1950–82).

Most of our available documentation dates from colonial times. Many of these address economic matters: some in Spanish, some in Nahuatl, and some with accompanying illustrations. There are on-the-spot letters and reports by *conquistadores*, as well as their recollections (Cortés, 1928; Díaz del Castillo, 2008; Fuentes, 1963); accounts of Aztec history and culture by Spanish ecclesiastics such as Diego Durán (1971, 1994) and Bernardino de Sahagún (1950–82); and native chronicles by, for instance, Fernando de Alva Ixtlilxochitl (1965) and Fernando Alvarado Tezozomoc (1975). Spaniards interested in making the most of their newly conquered lands undertook censuses of native communities, wrote official reports, and produced a plethora of legal and tax records. Meanwhile, everyday Indigenous people adapted to the new order and produced, in their native languages, documents such as wills, land claims, lawsuits, and complaints (Anderson et al., 1976).

This is a robust and diverse documentary record. It is also flawed. *Conquistadores* wrote self-serving and biased accounts, ecclesiastics were primarily interested in religious conversion, and Spaniards saw their encounters with this new world through Spanish eyes. Indigenous authors often had the promotion of their own city-state as a major motivation. Some matters, such as women's activities and the daily lives of slaves, are rarely addressed. Still, although the documentary record is incomplete and unbalanced, it is rich and diverse enough to allow us important insights into the Aztec economy.

But there is much more. Archaeological investigations fill in some of the documentary gaps. Available material evidence includes stationary constructions, portable objects (large and small, precious and ordinary), and human biological remains. There are vestiges of lofty temples, grand palaces, smaller houses, shrines, skull racks, ballcourts, warrior assembly rooms, schools, dams, terraces, and multitudinous ritual offerings. There are spectacular monuments. Carefully executed excavations and surveys have been undertaken in the Aztec heartland and in its provinces; those in ancient Tenochtitlan (today's downtown Mexico City) stand out. Numerous religious and civil structures in Tenochtitlan's sacred precinct have been fully or partially excavated and currently 209 ritual caches (containing, collectively, tens of thousands of artifacts) unearthed, greatly expanding our knowledge of the growth of the city and empire (López Austin and López Luján, 2009; López Luján, 2020). Archaeological investigations beyond the Aztec heartland offer perspectives from the conquered (e.g., Smith, 2017; Stark, 2017). Further inroads have been made through sophisticated analytical techniques that refine, for example, materials identification (e.g., Jansen et al., 2019) and sourcing (e.g., Millhauser et al., 2011; Thibodeau et al., 2018). Human remains add to our information assemblage, revealing data on the people themselves: their age and gender, nutrition, ills, occupations, movements, and manners of death (Chávez Balderas, 2020).

As a complement to the documentary record, archaeology serves as a significant and often rich source of information on the Aztec economy. But it too has its drawbacks. After the Spanish conquest, many buildings were leveled and their stones repurposed for Spanish buildings, and Spanish cities were built directly atop native ones (often making archaeological access all but impossible). Many types of objects such as paper and feathers are perishable and rarely survive the ravages of time. Many objects in museums lack useful provenience. Cremation was common, hampering the investigative efforts of bioarchaeologists.

But, on the positive side, there is still more. Today, there are more than two million speakers of the Nahuatl language and millions more who speak other Mesoamerican languages. Other aspects of Indigenous culture have also shown remarkable tenacity: Women still weave cloth on backstrap looms and grind maize on stone *metates*, people pound *Ficus* bark with stone bark beaters to make paper, and hoes and digging sticks are still used in agricultural fields. Sick persons consult *curanderos* and undergo traditional curing ceremonies, and people perform pilgrimages that embody many ancient practices (Sandstrom, 1991). The intervening 500 years have left their mark on the Indigenous cultures, and many of these technologies and traditions are hybrids (e.g., traditional hoes have steel tips and pilgrims may carry Cheetos on their treks). But enough has persisted to allow us a modern-day glimpse of some pre-Spanish technologies, customs, and beliefs.

1.4 Aims and Scope of this Element

This Element is a synthesis of the Aztec economic system during the last two centuries prior to Spanish contact. It favors no one theoretical posture; the approach here is unabashedly empirical. Collectively, the six sections that follow provide a comprehensive view of the many dimensions of the complex Aztec economy. This approach and organization allow for ease of comparison with other similar economies worldwide.

Section 2 discusses the domestic economy, recognizing that households were the basic units of production and consumption in Aztec society. Considered here are the varying types and scales of domestic economic organization as households secured access to resources, undertook production strategies, and faced opportunities, limitations, and restrictions on consumption. Section 3 covers the institutional economy, discussing economic dimensions of hierarchically arranged social, political, and religious institutions. Covered here are issues of land tenure, labor duties and mobilization, tribute/taxation impositions, palace support systems, special purpose levies, and temple service duties.

Section 4 moves on to economic specialization. Some specialists were full-time, others part-time. Some worked at home, others were attached to royal or noble palaces. Some worked voluntarily, others (like slaves) involuntarily. Economic interdependence was built in since few (if any) people produced all of their needs or perceived needs. This section naturally segues into Section 5: the highly commercialized Aztec economy. Merchants were pivotal actors in moving goods locally and throughout the imperial domain and beyond, markets were bustling and popular venues for exchanging virtually everything, supply and demand forces were at work, and commodity monies such as cacao beans and cotton cloaks facilitated exchanges. Gift exchanges were also instrumental in moving goods in a wide range of social, political, and religious contexts. Section 6 emphasizes changes over time in the Aztec economy, highlighting adjustments made to the changing conditions under imperial rule. Section 7 suggests productive future directions in studies of the Aztec economy. Reference entries provide more detailed and expansive discussions of all the matters treated in this Element.

2 Domestic Economy

Everywhere people eat. They sleep, raise children, work, and play. They are born and they die. They engage in rituals and enjoy social events. In the Aztec world, for most people, these daily, periodic, and occasional activities took place in households – some large, some small; some rich, some poor. Economically, households served as the primary units of production and consumption in Aztec society.

Household size and composition varied considerably throughout the Aztec domain. Houses ranged from large opulent palaces embracing polygynous families (with their entourages) and administrative offices, to smaller but still ample multiroom housing for extended families, and to more humble single-room dwellings most likely with nuclear families. Royal palaces were the grandest of all these. Those of the Mexica kings Ahuitzotl (r. 1486–1502) and Motecuhzoma Xocoyotzin (r. 1502–21) and the Texcocan king Nezahualcoyotl (r. 1418–72) were among the grandest of all. They served the ruler's administrative, military, and ritual needs (see Section 3.2.1). This was palace as government and showpiece. The ruler also enjoyed an expansive personal household with many wives, children, servants, and slaves all requiring a great many rooms for daily living, raising children, preparing and eating food, and performing household rituals. Rulers also had additional residences, pleasure palaces that served as royal retreats. All of these were expensively constructed with the very best materials and embellished with exquisite decorations – cloth awnings, wall hangings, mural paintings, and mosaics. Their domestic economies were oversized, whether in production, distribution, or consumption spheres. These were exceptional households but households nonetheless.

As a point of reference, royal palaces ranged in size from more than 2,000 to 25,000 square meters (Smith, 2008: 117). Known palaces of lesser nobles were considerably smaller, ranging from 200 to 540 square meters, suggesting that not all nobles were the same in wealth and status. Palaces overshadowed other dwellings in their cities and communities: Motecuhzoma Xocoyotzin's palace was apparently sixty times larger than commoner houses in Tenochtitlan. This was extraordinary. But even the noble palace in the much smaller city of Cihuatecpan was four times larger than other nearby houses in the community (Evans, 1991: 88). Excavated commoner houses throughout central Mexico ranged from several rooms arranged around a patio to single-room dwellings (Smith, 2008: 163–167; Figure 3). The former complexes could cover more than 400 square meters while the latter tended to provide around 20 square meters of indoor living space. Size alone can be a bit deceptive: Many daily activities took place out-of-doors, with the houses themselves used primarily for

Figure 3 Excavated commoner house. Photograph courtesy of Michael E. Smith.

storage, sleeping, and protection from the elements (Berdan, 2014: 63–64). Urban household compounds in Tenochtitlan itself were typically walled and contained "a number of separately entered dwelling units which faced inward on an open patio space" (Calnek, 1972: 111). These rooms varied in size and number; some were attached to *chinampa* fields, others were not. So, despite general patterns, pronounced variations in the footprints of residential sites point to obvious and almost individualized differences in the life circumstances of people we lump into the "commoner" category. There were prosperous and not-so-prosperous merchants, well-off and struggling artisans, and thriving and marginal farmers.

Household composition also varied. Nahuatl terminologies favor words denoting "the setting in which a joint life takes place, not the origin of the relationships between those living together" (Lockhart, 1992: 59). In other words, to the Aztecs themselves families were always significant, but in terms of living and working together, "household" was more operational than "family." Some of the larger houses and house complexes most likely contained multigenerational extended families and/or families with related and unrelated attached individuals. Such compounds were common in Tenochtitlan (Calnek, 1976), and specific documentary descriptions and depictions of urban Tenochtitlan and Tlatelolco residential sites reveal generally large and complex households that "tended to include descendants of 2–6 siblings" (Kellogg, 1988: 493). Individual households also experienced predictable life cycles and unpredictable events that affected their domestic compositions and social/economic strategies. Families with small children had more consumers than producers and tended to struggle economically more than those with more adolescent and adult laborers (Hirth, 2009a: 19). Frequent military campaigns took men away from home for a time or perhaps permanently, disrupting the gendered division of labor responsibilities in the household. Natural catastrophes were known to destroy crops and sometimes houses, requiring people to rebuild their lives elsewhere.

For some additional perspective, it is worthwhile noting what households were and what they were not. Traditional views of households typically describe them as self-sufficient, conservative, stable, unlikely to produce surpluses, manufacturing only utilitarian goods, and generally "a passive and inefficient unit of production" (Hirth, 2009a: 17). Aztec households were not. Instead, they were rarely if ever self-sufficient, they regularly produced surpluses, and they made both utilitarian and wealth goods. They were dynamic, flexible, adaptable, and innovative (Brumfiel, 1991; Hirth, 2009a: 17; Hirth, 2009b: 1).

The focus in this section is on economic strategies at this most fundamental level of social organization. This includes household production of food and crafts and the place of households in the larger Aztec economy. Emphasizing these processes and contexts carries the benefit of seeing how household economies worked, not just what they were.

2.1 Household Provisioning: Food

Rich or poor, urban or rural, people relied first and foremost on maize, beans, squashes, and chilis for food, all of which were available in many varieties (Figure 4). These mainstays were supplemented by a wide array of foods such as amaranth, chia, tomatoes, prickly pear pads and fruits, maguey sap, and avocados and other fruits; domesticated turkeys and dogs; and wild game, birds, fish, and insects. Flavorings featured vanilla, bees' honey, maguey sap, and chilis again. Seasonings such as salt and epazote were widely available. Cacao enhanced nobles' meals, tobacco aided digestion, mushrooms buoyed ceremonial feasts, and *pulque* from maguey provided an element of euphoria to certain ceremonies. Aromatic flowers (some consumed, some not) elevated the festive mood of special occasions. Households served as the primary units of organization for the production, distribution, and consumption of all of these.

Most food in the Aztec world was produced by agriculture, and most households were farming households. Basic staples and auxiliary plants were cultivated in *tierra caliente*, *tierra templada*, and *tierra fria*; along flatlands and on piedmont slopes; in dense forests and on treeless plateaus; and, notably,

Figure 4 Beans in a Mexican marketplace. Photograph by author.

alongside and within freshwater lakes. Farmers shared a general store of knowledge, skills, and tools (such as nature's signs for planting time and the ubiquitous digging stick) regardless of the agricultural environment. But they also made adaptations to specific conditions, tailoring varying techniques, technologies, and social arrangements to local ecologies and human needs. There are several ways of looking at the diverse agricultural systems within the Aztec domain. Among the most common are rainfall-dependent agriculture/ humidity-control cultivation (McClung de Tapia, 2000), extensive/intensive systems (e.g., Smith, 2012), and extensive seasonal/medium-intensive seasonal/intensive/special systems (Rojas Rabiela, 2001). I prefer this last scheme in that it implies more of a continuum of scale and casts the broadest net. It embraces the widely documented slash and burn systems of tropical rain forests; rainfall-fed fields with or without terracing (often incorporating short fallowing systems); irrigation using canals, dams, and other waterworks; lacustrine *chinampas*; and *calmilli* or *callalli*, garden plots located adjacent to people's residences.

In terms of the distribution of these systems within the Aztec imperial domain, the long fallowing slash and burn systems tend to be found in *tierra caliente*, in the more distant corners of the empire (and those conquered toward the end of the empire's history), while the rainfall-fed and irrigation systems were largely carried out in *templada* and *fria* zones. The northern and drier parts of the Basin of Mexico and beyond were particularly amenable to rainfall-fed and often terraced maguey cultivation. Where geographically and technologically suitable, irrigation augmented natural rainfall and allowed farmers to plant earlier in the year to harvest crops before the arrival of potentially damaging frosts. Irrigation also staved off low-rainfall periods and afforded greater food security than provided by rainfall alone.

Chinampas, sometimes erroneously called floating gardens, were rectangular fields constructed in shallow freshwater lake beds. These agricultural plots were especially common in the southern spring-fed lakes of the Basin of Mexico and along the western edge of Tenochtitlan, where fresh waters were walled off from the eastern saline Lake Texcoco by a series of effective dikes. *Chinampas* typically ranged from around two to four meters wide and twenty to forty meters long (Parsons, 1991: 21) and were arranged parallel to one another with canals separating the individual plots. Tenochtitlan *chinampas* characteristically were bordered on one side by a canal and on the other by a walkway (Calnek, 1972: 109). *Chinampa* plots were farmed by individual households whose members often worked seven nearby or attached fields (Cline, 1986). Their high, sustained productivity was achieved through multicropping, crop rotation, the use of staggered seedbeds, nutrient and water replenishment from adjacent canals, and intensive labor commitments. Under these conditions, crops including maize, beans, tomatoes, amaranth, chilis, and various greens, herbs, and ornamentals thrived. Household garden plots (*calmilli* or *callalli*) were common in both urban and rural settings. They were located alongside houses where both labor and household refuse for fertilizer were conveniently available; domesticated turkeys and dogs also provided natural fertilizing. Planting on *calmilli* was opportunistic and situational: maize, vegetables, herbs, medicines, and ornamentals might be planted, whether for immediate household needs, social and ceremonial exchanges, or trading in the marketplace.

People supplemented their diets by engaging in other food-getting pursuits such as tending domesticated animals, hunting, gleaning, fishing, and salt production. Most turkeys and dogs were raised in household settings. They could also be obtained in marketplaces, for a price: In Tlaxcalla in 1545, a turkey cock cost 200 cacao beans, a turkey hen cost 100, and a turkey egg could be purchased for 3 cacao beans. For perspective, a tamale or twenty small tomatoes cost one cacao bean (Anderson et al., 1976: 211). If raised at home, turkeys consumed some of the household stores of maize, tortillas, tamales, chilis, and greens, and dogs ate maize and meat (Sahagún, 1950–82, book 10: 54, 16).

Wild animals and plants were also on the Aztec menu. They hunted deer, hares, rabbits, armadillos, gophers and other small rodents, reptiles and amphibians, and birds; they collected insects, honey, aquatic algae (*Spirulina*), and salt. Deer were hunted with bows and arrows, and other animals were usually snared in nets. Small birds were brought down with blowguns, and other birds, especially waterfowl, were captured in nets and snares (Berres, 2000: 34–35; Sahagún, 1950–82, book 8: 30; book 11: 49). Swarms of locusts offered opportunities for collection in the fall. Salt was produced in the saline northern-most lakes of the Basin "by collecting salty earth, leaching it, and boiling the resulting brine" (Parsons, 2001: 158). In the Basin of Mexico, fish and other aquatic fauna were caught on hooks-and-lines, with spears, with handheld nets from canoes (Figure 5), and with seine nets (Berres, 2000: 32–33). With the possible exception of the seine net procedures, these food-getting activities could be pursued with labor and technologies available at the single household level. The qualities of numerous wild plants were well-known and gleaned broadly for food, flavorings, and medicines.

Once acquired, foods had to be processed, preserved, stored, prepared, and served up. Maize was shelled and the best seed separated out for the next planting. The remainder of the maize was stored inside the house or outside in special-purpose granaries, with vermin ever-present threats. Everyone in the realm ate maize daily, and its preparation took place in virtually every household. The kernels were soaked and boiled in an alkaline solution (such as wood ashes or a piece of limestone) overnight, ground into a meal (*masa*) with a *mano* and *metate* the next morning, and then patted into *tortillas* and cooked on a flat griddle (*comalli*). Alternatively, the ground maize could be formed into *tamales* or mixed with water to make *atolli*, a thick, nutritious drink. The many different kinds of tortillas were combined with just about every other food – especially beans but also chilis, honey, prickly pear cactus fruit, water fly eggs, and whatever was available at the moment. Tamales were especially popular for festive occasions and featured a wide range of other foods grown or otherwise obtained by household members: There were fish tamales, cooked bean tamales, frog tamales, red fruit tamales, turkey egg tamales, and so on. Some dishes, with maize, beans, turkey and dog meat, along with other foods and seasonings were cooked as stews in pots (Berdan and Anawalt, 1992, vol. 3, folios 61r, 68r). Numerous varieties of chilis were ground up and added spice to any meal (Coe, 1994; Sahagún, 1950–82, book 10: 67, 69, 80; book 9: 37). All households were stocked with a standard inventory of cooking equipment and serving wares: grinding stones, mortars and pestles, griddles, grater bowls, pots of different sizes and shapes, baskets, cups, bowls, and plates. These varied in style and quality and were available in marketplaces, if not produced in the household itself.

Figure 5 Fourteen-year-old boy fishing and girl weaving. Berdan and Anawalt (1992, vol. 4: folio 60r).

Some households augmented their daily maize regimen with more specialized food production. For instance, if maguey processing was a major domestic enterprise, household members also spent a great deal of time producing sap, syrup, and fermented *pulque*, in addition to steaming and scraping the leaves and extracting fibers from them (Evans, 2005: 206–207). Farther afield, cacao growers not only picked the cacao pods; they also separated the beans from the pulp, laid the beans out to ferment, and then dried and roasted them. They then packed them up for trade (counting them carefully) or ground them up for their own pleasure. Still, in these and other specialized food-producing households, maize was still the dietary mainstay.

The focus here is on the importance of food in household economies and therefore with matters such as labor requirements and inputs, social and ceremonial contexts, scheduling, technological investments, and food distribution. All agricultural (and other food-getting) work was labor-intensive, with men the primary workers in the fields. However, women, older children, and sometimes other (nonresident) workers went to the fields during high-activity times such as harvest. Women's work was characteristically tied to home and hearth; their umbilical cords were buried by the hearth, symbolizing their lifelong attachment to household activities such as cooking, weaving, and caring for children. Therefore, women were most available for farm work when fields were close to houses, which was common in both rural and urban areas (Smith, 2012: 75–77). Women's daily activities could quite readily incorporate tasks such as forming seed beds in *chinampas* and tending domesticated turkeys and dogs and the array of edible, medicinal, and ornamental plants in garden house plots (for more on household division of labor, see Brumfiel, 1991).

Children contributed to the household economy at an early age. The *Codex Mendoza* (Berdan and Anawalt, 1992, vol. 3: folios 58r–60r) shows boys toting water at age four, with their household chores growing yearly with their strength and abilities: carrying firewood at age five, accompanying their fathers to the marketplace at age six, and learning to fish at age seven. During those years, girls learned how to spin thread, although they surely were also helping around the house. Beginning at age eight, the *Codex Mendoza* shifts from skill acquisition to punishments, picking up the children again at ages thirteen and fourteen when boys are by then adept at fishing and girls are fully capable cooks and weavers. While this document depicts a fishing lifestyle, age-related tasks can be translated into other food-getting enterprises; in mid-twentieth-century Tepoztlan in Morelos, Nahua boys began helping their fathers in the fields by age six, by age seven girls were helping their mothers with household tasks, and by age nine girls had mastered grinding maize, making tortillas, and cooking other foods (Lewis, 1951: 100). These were all hugely time-consuming tasks, requiring, for instance, four to six hours each day for grinding maize by hand (Lewis, 1951: 99). Household compounds with separate living spaces suggest that these compounds typically could mobilize multiple persons of both genders for shared and cooperative labor such as this.

Food acquisition and preparation activities intensified at the onset of particular ritual and social events, including some of the monthly ceremonies that customarily included feasting. Maize, turkeys, chilis, and available vegetables and fruits were almost universally consumed at social and ritual feasts and were "cooked and otherwise prepared, invariably, in individual households (whether noble or commoner)" (Berdan, 2017: 134). Offerings included, for instance, snakes, flowers, and tamales during the month of Toçoztontli, quail during Toxcatl, and amaranth dough formed into little hills during Tepeihuitl. Men enthusiastically hunted deer during the autumn month of Quecholli when the deer were their fattest (Durán, 1971). Most statewide ceremonies included a household component such as making tamales, stringing flowers, or feasting. Other rituals requiring food were largely performed in households, especially those pertaining to life-cycle celebrations.

All food-getting strategies involved some degree of seasonality; farmers' schedules responded to distinct wet-and-dry seasons, life cycles of individual plants and animals, technological requirements, and social/ceremonial demands like those already mentioned. The winter dry season was a usual "down time" in many agricultural households, when people could pursue other activities. Winter also saw the arrival of millions of edible migratory birds to the Basin of Mexico lakes, and low water levels at that same time were optimal for salt collection (Gibson, 1964: 141–142, 338). Agricultural pursuits varied considerably in their extent of technological investment, although the basic cultivating tool kit was likely manufactured and repaired widely. Terraces, dams, canals, *chinampas*, and other hydraulic and earth works demanded year-round time commitments for maintenance and repairs, although they experienced some ups and downs in scheduling. Imbalances and fluctuations in production schedules were negotiated by household and multi-household pooling, gift exchanges, and marketplace transactions. Household economic security was also enhanced by taking on additional productive activities – notably crafts.

2.2 Household Provisioning: Crafts

Aztec households characteristically produced more than food. At the very least, all adult women spun thread and wove cloth. Beyond these consequential contributions by approximately half of the adult population, household economic strategies often included the production of other crafts, whether utilitarian or luxury.

In general, crafting and multicrafting provided a buttress against nonproductive times in food-getting, diversified household economies, and helped households minimize risk in its short-term and long-term provisioning. It also could be harmonized with seasonal agricultural and other domestic schedules. In particular, multicrafting "enables artisans to reduce risk by producing a repertoire of products with different value, demand, and consumer consumption cycles" (Hirth, 2009a: 22). Furthermore, household crafting was intermittent (discontinuous or periodic), filling in scheduling gaps and complementing other economic activities. Crafting was clearly important, but what (and to what degree) did crafts contribute to domestic success and well-being? How did crafting fit into the overall household economy?

The production of crafts in domestic settings can be glimpsed through a brief foray into three representative crafts: cloth, pottery, and feather works. These included things that everybody used and things that only some people used; some were utilitarian and others were luxury; all required the development of specialized skills.

Everybody wore clothing, so it is not surprising that cloth production was the most ubiquitous craft in Mesoamerica. In addition to clothing, woven cloth was used for deity adornments, awnings and decorative hangings, nighttime coverings, tortilla covers, funerary wraps, marriage payments, ritual gifts, and money. Spinning and weaving were learned by all women whether noble or commoner, rich or poor, urban or rural, and regardless of geographic location. Women manufactured textiles almost entirely from cotton and from leaf fibers, particularly maguey (Figures 5 and 6).

First, cotton. Cotton, of several varieties, grew only in lowland regions – coastal areas and inland valleys primarily below 1,000 meters in elevation. Yet women throughout the Aztec domain, including those in highland regions, produced cotton cloth. Lively trade networks and widespread marketplaces made cotton available everywhere and also served as outlets for the weavers' production. Essential tools consisted of wooden sticks (of different sizes and shapes); whorls typically of clay or wood; small ceramic or gourd spinning bowls; and picks of bone, maguey spines, or other convenient material. Other materials that may or may not have been employed included dyes, small feathers, and rabbit fur. Depending on the household's location and resources, these may have been provided in-house or purchased in a nearby marketplace. One enticing archaeological find, in Cholula, comprised "a bone whorl, a spindle-whorl mold, a ceramic vessel filled with powdered dye, bone tools, and deer antlers" (McCafferty and McCafferty, 2000: 42).

Hand spinning with a spindle and whorl and weaving with a backstrap loom are often characterized as "simple" technologies, the loom described as only a "bundle of sticks," a term I admit to having used myself (Berdan, 2014: 24). Yet this is misleading in two ways. First, a stick is not just a stick. There were (and are) warp beams, breast beams, heddles, and the prized batten (or weaving

Figure 6 Modern-day Nahua woman weaving. Photograph by author.

sword). Some years ago, I met a woman in the Sierra Norte de Puebla who wove with the most gorgeous, shiny smooth batten; she told me that she had let her daughters know, in no uncertain terms, that she wished to be buried with it. It was her most valuable possession. Second, the skills were (and are) complex and take time and dedication to acquire, as part of a girl's broader practical and moral education (Hendon, 2006: 362–363). The *Codex Mendoza* indicates that a girl mastered weaving by age fourteen (Berdan and Anawalt, 1992, vol. 3: folio 60r), a detail confirmed in my ethnographic interviews. The *Codex Mendoza* does not tell us when a girl began learning the skill, but today's weavers in the Sierra Norte de Puebla have told me that they began at age five; it is reasonable to project that back in time. A good ten years to gain proficiency is no small commitment. So, part of the household's energy, in this case that of adult women, was dedicated to teaching this craft to the next generation of girls.

Aztec (and Mesoamerican) styles of spinning and weaving fit conveniently into other female domestic duties. Spindle and loom were easily picked up and dropped and readily integrated into other daily activities whether cooking, caring for children, sweeping the floor, tending the household garden, going to market, or chatting with a visitor. And like these expected female tasks, producing cloth was a year-round activity, although occasionally interrupted by extra-ordinary events such as a major ceremony, the birth of a child, or an unexpected illness. Some women, such as midwives, had additional demands on their time. There were labor advantages to living in extended households, with more than one adult woman at hand. Of course, noble polygynous households could produce many times the amount of cloth than commoner households; it is likely that they manufactured more highly decorated, and hence more highly valued, cloth. Priestesses, also, spent much of their time in cloth production.

The creation of maguey textiles entailed somewhat different household arrangements. Maguey thrived in "essentially the high, semi-arid plains and hill flanks of central and north-central Mexico, centering on the Valley of Mexico" and spreading out into adjacent upland regions of *tierra fria* (Parsons and Parsons, 1990: 3). While maguey and maize cultivation often occurred together, maguey exploitation could be successful in more marginal lands where maize cultivation was risky. These versatile plants provided food (*pulque*, sap, sugar, vinegar, and leaf flesh), fibers, construction materials, fuel, paper, medicine, and miscellaneous household and artisanal conveniences (e.g., as surfaces for feather working). Fibers were used in the production of fine and coarse textiles, cordage, sandals, and carrying bags. Production and processing of these materials relied on specialized tool kits, techniques, and knowledge and were ongoing during the year: The multipurpose nature of maguey lent itself to domestic multicrafting. While it may seem as though there would have been little room for taking on additional crafting activities in such households, at least one maguey fiber household workshop in Otompan diversified further and also made "cotton and maguey spindle whorl molds and spindle whorls, basalt scrapers to process maguey, as well as doing some lapidary working" (Hirth and Nichols, 2017: 291).

Unlike maize agriculture, maguey cultivation was a year-round activity (Figure 7). Individual plants reached maturity from seven to twenty-five years, and only about 2–7 percent of a farmer's plants would be producing sap (*aguamiel*) at any one time, each plant exuding sap for two to six months (Parsons and Parsons, 1990: 18). Collecting the sap was labor-intensive, as was its transformation into *pulque*, sugar, and other consumables. Harvesting the leaves for fiber was likewise labor-intensive and not seasonally restrictive. Extracting both sap and fibers likely took place in households located close to the fields: The sap had a short "shelf life" and the leaves were heavy and cumbersome. Spinning and weaving of maguey fibers by women were domestic tasks. Like their cotton-using sisters, these women used spindles and whorls for spinning and backstrap looms for weaving; the whorls were larger and they did

Figure 7 Maguey plant. Photograph by author.

not need the little spinning bowls, but the technology and learning processes were essentially the same. There may have been some crossover in cotton and maguey fiber spinning; in excavations at Cihuatecpan, Evans (2005: 218–219) found that "in all households women were spinning both cotton and maguey." Overall, extended households provided a good fit where so many activities were going on at once (Evans, 2005; Parsons and Parsons, 1990: 335). However, this may not have been the only arrangement for producing maguey textiles. Nichols et al. (2000: 284) argue for maguey-fiber workshops in Otompan that "processed maguey, made spindle whorls, spun thread of various sizes, including cordage, and perhaps cloth was woven and dyed," with these concentrated in specific districts or *calpolli*. And perhaps there were other combinations of activities, other workable strategies, yet to be discovered.

Everybody also used pottery. Every household needed containers, cooking wares, serving wares, and spinning equipment: basins, jars, pots, bowls, grater bowls, griddles, plates, cups, spinning bowls, and spindle whorls (Figure 8). Braziers, musical instruments, stamps, molds, and religious objects (notably censers and figurines) also were fashioned from clay.

The *Florentine Codex* describes the clay worker as "a dealer in clay objects" and lists a wide repertoire of utilitarian ceramics laid out on his market mat. The griddle (*comalli*) maker likewise sold his wares in the market (Sahagún, 1950–82, book 10: 83) but separately from the general pottery maker/vendor. How did the "generalist" operate? Consider a few possible options: A single pottery-making household might make only bowls (or other object) and sell them in the market. Or a household may make, say, bowls, jars, and basins at

Figure 8 Tripod bowl. Courtesy National Museum of the American Indian, Smithsonian Institution, no. 027169. Photograph by Jennifer Berdan Lozano.

the same time or in sequence and sell them in individual or separate lots. Or a potter might market products made by his neighboring potters, much as he might give his products to a market-going neighbor. Or any of several other permutations – household crafting was creative, opportunistic, and flexible.

Pottery making required several steps and a particular tool kit, all of which could be effectively provided by households. One must obtain appropriate clays, which were widely available (Neff et al., 2000: 307), mix the clay with plant fibers or other materials (for temper), and then form the desired object by beating it into shape, coiling, or molding with clay molds (which themselves must be manufactured) (Minc, 2017: 361–362). The objects were then dried, decorated (perhaps polished with a smooth stone or stick, perhaps painted), and fired. Firing typically took place on the house lot in a pit or on the ground whereby "pots are stacked and covered by a layer of brush or kindling and the whole set on fire" (Minc, 2017: 364). All of this could be (and was) accomplished with household resources – tools, labor, space, and knowledge.

In some cases, pottery making (and other crafts) became concentrated in residential districts (*calpolli*) and cities (Nichols, 1994). The community of Otompan, in the northeastern corner of the Basin of Mexico, is a case in point. There, archaeologists have discovered a clay workers' barrio of "clustered households engaged in the production of mold-made figurines, spindle whorls, earspools, musical instruments, and stamps, as well as simple domestic bowls" (Minc, 2017: 365). In the same community, residents of a more elite neighborhood manufactured long-handled censers used in rituals (Hirth and Nichols, 2017: 288; Minc, 2017: 365). The censers appear to have been consumed locally, while figurines were marketed more broadly (Hirth and Nichols, 2017: 290, 292; Neff et al., 2000: 320). Spatially concentrated or dispersed, locally used or more widely distributed, these activities were carried out in domestic settings.

Pots broke much as clothing wore out. There was almost endless demand for these products and, with Aztec-period population growth, demand must have been on the upswing. Feather working was a somewhat different matter, effectively targeting a more restricted (albeit also growing) group of consumers: rulers, nobles, priests, rich merchants, and valiant warriors. Fancy feathered objects served these high-ranking or accomplished people as symbols of status, power, and wealth. They bedecked kings as they publicly performed their political and religious duties. They were presented to warriors in recognition of their battlefield achievements. They adorned deities, litters, celebrants, and environs in public ceremonies; dazzling, luminescent, flowing feathers added rhythm and flowing movements to processions and dances. These stunning objects included banners, fans, headpieces, headdresses, arm and leg bands, textiles (especially capes, tunics, and decorative hangings), warrior costumes, back devices, and shields. Although this was a luxury craft, it nonetheless took place in domestic settings.

Feathered objects required low-value feathers as well as exotic, high-value feathers (from birds such as scarlet macaws, lovely cotingas, roseate spoon-bills, hummingbirds, various parrots, and the prized quetzal). Depending on their current project, feather workers also required auxiliary materials, all of which were fairly cheap and widely available: unspun cotton, cotton thread, and cotton cloth; maguey paper, twines, and leaves; animal hides; obsidian blades; bone picks; glues; dyes; wood and reed sticks; ceramic vats and bowls; and baskets.

Feather workers used these materials and tools to produce objects that were predominately mosaics (like shields), tied adornments (like banners and head-dresses), or embellished textiles (such as capes and warrior costumes). While whole objects are sometimes characterized by one of these techniques, almost all were hybrids. For instance, the quetzal feather headdress in Vienna combines tying and mosaic making; the surface of the coyote shield in that same city is a mosaic, but numerous tied feathers dangle from its rim (see Berdan, 2014: 100–102).

Techniques and procedures were complicated and required dedicated training and meticulous workmanship (see Berdan and Smith, 2021: 68–74; Filloy and Moreno Guzmán, 2017; Sahagún, 1950–82, book 9: 91–97). Divisions of labor and careful coordination of activities were essential within the feather-working household. Men were the primary artisans, managing the operation and engaging in most stages of production. Women sorted and dyed feathers. Girls helped their mothers with sorting, being trained from an early age to perceive the slightest variations in colors. Boys made glues. All household members were engaged in the enterprise, adding these tasks to their usual chores around the house. Work patterns were ongoing (e.g., selecting and dyeing feathers), sequential (e.g., precious feathers necessarily laid atop cheaper dyed ones), and on call (e.g., making glues that must be used promptly). The household's master feather worker oversaw the projects, assigning duties, coordinating activities, and assuring that his high standards were met. He also negotiated with other artisans who contributed to the enterprise: scribes drew the initial patterns, and most feathered objects were adorned with gold or precious stones that were specifically designed and supplied by those artisans. So, we hear of now-lost finery such as "a feather piece, the center blue with stone mosaic work, with other colored feathers, the border of green feathers, and lined with a jaguar skin" and a shield with "the field red with some fancy work of gold" (Saville 1920: 62, 72) in the sixteenth century inventories of wealth sent from Mexico to Spain. Given that any one object combined mosaic work, tying, and the attachment of gold or stone embellishments, the most efficient feather-working households would have contained members that were trained, capable, and experienced in all of these techniques.

It is not clear how the manufacture of feathered textiles fit into these arrangements and routines. There are some suggestions that very small feathers were spun (perhaps intertwined with cotton) using tiny spindles, the threads then woven into ultrafine cloth (Berdan and Smith, 2021: 71; McCafferty and McCafferty, 2000: 47). Noblewomen were engaged in spinning feathers in Motecuhzoma Xocoyotzin's palace, but also commoner women spun the feathers of ordinary birds in the Tlatelolco marketplace. Perhaps women of feather-working households also spun and wove feathered textiles – the skills and materials would have been immediately available to them.

There were, of course, many other types of crafts. Householders made obsidian blades, paper, brooms, dyes, smoking tubes, reed baskets and mats, rubber balls, mirrors, shiny gourd bowls . . . the list goes on and on. Households incorporated these production activities as strategies to enhance their well-being and reduce risk. Their choice of craft was conditioned by factors such as access to raw materials, availability of appropriate labor and skills, scheduling arrangements, and outlets for the finished product. Different crafts demanded different degrees of economic investment, usually in raw materials – the feather worker, lapidary, and gold worker produced "luxury" objects of materials defined as precious, expensive, and exotic; utilitarian artisans such as basket and sandal makers worked in less expensive and more broadly accessible raw materials. In whatever case, the tools were often cheap and widely available and were often general-purpose household implements.

Households often depended on multicrafting and/or reliable commodity chains (Millhauser and Overholtzer, 2020). For instance, thread spinning required mold-made pottery whorls that could be made in-house, purchased in a marketplace, gifted from a generous neighbor, or perhaps inherited. Feather workers most likely purchased obsidian blades, dyes, maguey materials, and animal hides; they made orchid glues in-house but probably purchased the orchid root powder in the marketplace – it was sold at least in Tlatelolco (Sahagún, 1950–82, book 10: 87). These and a multitude of other instances highlight the degree to which households were integrated into larger economic frameworks: They could pool and share resources and labor with their neighbors, deal with traveling merchants, trade in marketplaces, and/or enjoy a royal sponsorship.

2.3 Households in the Larger Aztec Economy

Households cooperated with each other economically in several ways: They exchanged labor at peak production times, shared resources in common economic pursuits, and gathered together and pooled their resources for essential social and ritual events. Consider these few examples. Labor exchanges occur in twentieth-century Mexican agricultural communities at "critical points in the crop growing cycle" (Sandstrom, 1991: 313; see also Kelly and Palerm, 1952; Lewis, 1951). It is reasonable to project these types of arrangements back in time. Professional merchants (*pochteca*) carried the goods of their *pochteca* neighbors on their long and dangerous trading expeditions (Sahagún, 1950–82, book 9: 14). Inter-craft collaborations were the rule among luxury artisans such as the feather workers who depended on the contributions of scribes, gold workers, and lapidaries in producing their feathered masterpieces, and residential clustering of some crafts in Otompan "facilitated a high degree of interdependence among industries" (Nichols 1994: 184). Reciprocity was an integral part of the major ceremonies. At the domestic level, this entailed cross-household ritual sharing of food and gifts (e.g., Sahagún, 1950–82, book 2: 84, 95, 147, 149, 167). Life-cycle rituals such as babies' naming ceremonies, dedications of children to school or temple, and weddings customarily called for the sharing of food and giving of gifts across households (Berdan and Anawalt, 1992, vol. 3: folios 56v, 61r; Durán, 1971: 123–124, 406, 424; Sahagún, 1950–82, book 6: 129, 209). Ceremonial events often required participation by people from all households or a selection of them by residence, gender, age, or occupation. There were situations where many individuals consumed large quantities of the same materials at the same time, such as when women performed synchronized dances in the streets with little red feathers pasted on their arms and legs.

Householders dealt with traveling merchants and in marketplaces for the whole spectrum of necessities and luxuries, from foods to medicines and from gold to slaves. Of course, professional merchants were specialist householders themselves who needed to eat and dress, and people selling in marketplaces were most often the very same householders that have been the subject of this section: farmers and artisans. Indeed, most marketplace vendors were producers of the products and wares they hawked (see Section 5).

Some households were attached to royal or other noble palaces and by that very circumstance were necessarily tied to broader economic processes. These included at least metal workers, feather workers, painters, stone cutters, lapidaries, and wood carvers, as well as *pulque* makers. Their high-end and other essential materials would have been available in the palace storehouses, stocked by tribute or other assessments (see Section 3). There was no ambiguity as to their customers: They worked specifically for their royal or noble sponsors.

Some aspects of these relationships were predictable, others were not. Highly predictable were the monthly ceremonies, which required broad participation and specific material outlays: Flower vendors could expect an onslaught of customers during the month of Tlaxochimaco, and potters would increase their production prior to widespread feasting. Fast-food vendors from individual households could expect brisk business on most days. Yet expectations were not always met. Farmers relied on predicting the onset of rains, but droughts or an early frost could spell disaster for their crops. Luxury artisans dependent on exotic materials obtained by professional merchants might face supply issues as the merchants were delayed due to weather or war, or worse yet, assassinated on the road. Some things were simply beyond the control of individual householders.

Much as household economies were flexible, so too were the strategic decisions made by householders concerning their external relations. What part of our harvest should we consume, what part should we save for the next seeding, and what part should we trade for other needed goods? Should we eat the turkey for this month's feast or save her for producing eggs? And what about fixing the stone terrace – should I call in help from my neighbor or redeem that obligation when a more dire need might arise? These and innumerable other decisions were made in the context of individual domestic settings, at the same time recognizing the opportunities and limitations presented by the broader economic world. Householders flowed with and adjusted to dynamic situations, whether a natural disaster, the vagaries of warfare, or the balancing of their interests with those of other groups in the society.

3 Institutional Economy

In the Aztec world, social, political, and religious institutions were arranged hierarchically. They were integrated and materially supported through well-established economic mechanisms and rooted in access to and allocation of land and labor. These economic mechanisms included palace support systems, rotational labor drafts (corvée), tribute/taxation impositions, special purpose levies, and temple service duties. In addition, feasting and gift-giving events moved goods about, sent social and political messages, and, at the highest levels, cemented elite alliances and terrified enemies. Materials and goods channeled in the institutional economy impacted production, distribution, and consumption arrangements in the imperial heartland as well as in outlying provinces.

3.1 Land and Labor

Land and labor were the cornerstones of the Aztec economy. They provided the bases for all production activities, from essential foods to utilitarian goods, luxury items, buildings, and waterworks. Land and labor also served to integrate people and institutions up and down the social and political scales.

3.1.1 Land

Landholding adhered to principles of hierarchy, with power concentrated in the person and office of the *tlatoani* (ruler). Each city-state had its own hereditary *tlatoani*, and it was he (or more rarely, she) who had ultimate rights to land and its allocation. To Hicks (1986: 49), "The general pattern, at least in the Valley of Mexico, was that land was assigned by the ruler to the royal palace, a noble house, or one or another state institution (including the temples) and was inherited thereafter." While this sounds direct and straightforward, there were complexities, ambiguities, and nuances (and not just to modern scholars but perhaps to the Aztecs themselves). Debate has raged for decades: Lands were owned personally by nobles; no, lands were attached to political offices. The *calpolli* owned lands and allocated them out to their residents; no, nobles held all the lands and disposed of them at will. Land could be sold; no, it could not. Land was held communally; well, yes and no. These are complicated and long-winded issues, so here I briefly present the current thinking on the subject and offer a helpful selection of references.

Lands appear under several designations, most referring to ownership or control. There were those that seem to have been the prerogative of titled nobles themselves. Farmers directly attached to individual nobles worked their lands and owed regular material tributes and labor duties to their overlords. These lands would include lands called *tlatocatlalli* (ruler's land), *tecpantlalli* (palace land), and *pillalli* (noble's land) according to Alva Ixtlilxochitl (1965: 170). But few things are simple: Torquemada (1969, vol. 2: 545–546) distinguishes two types of *pillalli*. He describes both as private property, but one type was the patrimonial land of kings and lords with dependent workers; the other constituted rewards to deserving nobles but lacked attached laborers. Both types could be inherited or sold. It appears that, as Lockhart (1992: 108) suggests, "noblemen's holdings were a world in themselves."

Alva Ixtlilxochitl (1965: 170) also mentions *calpollalli* (*calpolli* land) and *altepetlalli* (*altepetl* land), lands belonging to neighborhoods and towns. Residents cultivated these lands for their own sustenance and to meet their tribute payments. According to Lockhart (1992: 146), "the bulk of the arable land was held and worked by individuals and households." The individuals and households mentioned by Lockhart had access to lands by virtue of their membership in a particular *calpolli* and, by extension, an *altepetl*, both of whom were "deeply involved with landholding" (Lockhart, 1992: 146). These social and political units appear to have managed lands allocated to them by nobles: I agree with most scholars today that commoners could not own land; land came to them from a local noble landowner (Smith and Hicks, 2017: 426). Individual farmers were allocated plots by the local leadership; as long as they retained their *calpolli* and *altepetl* memberships and continued to work their plots, farmers were assured of perpetual use of these lands, which they could pass on to their heirs (Lockhart, 1992; Morehart, 2017; Smith and Hicks, 2017).

There were many more types of land as well – for example, *teopantlalli* (temple land), *yaotlalli* or *milchimalli* (war or military land; perhaps conquest lands), *tequitlalli* (tribute land), *huehuetlalli* (old or patrimonial land), *cihuatlalli* (women's land), and *tlalcohualli* (purchased land). These seem to designate particularities such as land use or means of acquisition. Temple lands were dedicated to temple maintenance and priestly support. War lands were those acquired from vanquished foes and/or farmed for military support. Tribute lands were dedicated to tribute payments. Women's lands were perhaps acquired as dowries. Purchased land was obtained through sale, although there is some question about how common this was in pre-Spanish times (Cline, 1984; Hicks, 1986; Hirth, 2016: 35–39; Lockhart, 1992: 155–163). A single noble's estate could contain lands of several different kinds. As an example, the Oztoticpac Lands Map details the estate and lands of an Indigenous noble in the environs of Texcoco; his lands were acquired through inheritance, gifts, patrimony, and purchase. The estate included commoners' lands (*calpollalli*) and lands worked by renters who owed a portion of their proceeds to their overlord (Harvey,

1991). Although the map dates from almost twenty years after the Spanish conquest, it likely reflects more ancient patterns and exemplifies the multifaceted nature of the landholding system.

This was the situation in the Basin of Mexico and environs, but regional diversity needs to be taken into account when looking more broadly at the Aztec world (see Harvey, 1984; Hirth, 2016: 39–41; Johnson, 2018). For instance, to the east in the Tlaxcallan region, "the land was held collectively by the *tecalli* [noble house], which was governed by a high lord," and *calpolli* were virtually nonexistent (Smith and Hicks, 2017: 426). Commoners gained access to farming lands by virtue of their residence in a village controlled by a *tecalli*; in exchange for this use, they provided their overlord with specified goods and services.

Land ownership and control were complicated by the dynamic relations among city-states and the fluid nature of population movements in Aztec times. Lands of vanquished city-states were often seized in wars of conquest and granted to the victorious: kings, deserving nobles, valiant warriors, and loyal communities and allies could all be granted these lands. For example, when the Mexica and their allies overthrew Azcapotzalco, its lands were distributed to the victors based on hierarchical principles and battlefield contributions: The best lands went to the king and his royal house, then ten "pieces of land" to the Mexica second-in-command, two pieces each to nobles who fought in the war, and lastly one piece to each participating *calpolli* for support of their god; commoners who had performed extraordinary feats were also given lands (Durán, 1994: 82–83). A similar pattern was followed in the aftermath of victorious wars with other Basin of Mexico city-states such as Coyoacan, Xochimilco, and Chalco (Durán, 1994: 101–103, 112–113, 148). Undoubtedly, the local farmers continued to work the lands, but a share of the harvest now would be due to their new nonresident landlords. All of this led to a patchwork of land ownership deeply rooted in conquest histories. To look at just one case, the lands acquired from the war with Azcapotzalco had earlier been taken and reallocated from other city-states in Azcapotzalco's own prior wars and undoubtedly had been shuffled about from even earlier wars. This was the case all over the Basin of Mexico and surely beyond (Hodge, 1991). In a hypothetical scenario, what had once been a plot of *tecpantlalli* became *pillalli* and then *calpollalli* and then *pillalli* and so on. Some of these very plots might also end up as *teopantlalli* or *cihuatlalli*. The designations were situational, changeable, and fluid. The biography of a single plot of land would be interesting indeed!

With so many conquests, how did the Mexica and their allies manage this apparently unwieldy and sprawling landholding system? We have one description, by Durán (1994: 129), that stewards and overseers were "placed on the lands belonging to the crown. They were to be responsible for cultivating them, improving them, gathering the crops and storing these in the royal warehouses." The king might be able to administer in this fashion, but it is not known exactly how an absentee noble or neighborhood managed their lands. Landholding administration was especially complicated since a single land-holder could hold lands in widely dispersed and unconnected areas. Lands of city-states conquered beyond the Basin of Mexico by the Mexica and their allies do not appear to have been divided in this fashion, but if governors or garrisons were imposed, local lands were typically set aside for support of those installations (Berdan et al., 1996).

To add to the complexities, there was a great deal of population movement in Aztec times – people were displaced in wars and sought survival during dire droughts and famines. Groups large and small sought new lives beyond their own homelands and requested lands or other types of situations in established communities. Such was the well-recorded history of the Mexica in their own migration into the Basin of Mexico as they sought sanctuary here and there (Berdan, 2014: 37–42). Apparently, refugees were often welcomed and absorbed. For instance, the Huexotzincas, harassed by their Tlaxcallan neighbors, sought asylum in Tenochtitlan in the early sixteenth century. The Mexica themselves coped with severe drought in the mid-fifteenth century, moving (under duress) to the Gulf Coast and the productive lands of the Totonac peoples. When the drought ended, some returned but others remained on the coast.

3.1.2 Labor

The Aztec economy was labor-intensive. Men farmed with hoes and digging sticks; women ground maize on stone *metates* and wove cloth on backstrap looms. Pottery and baskets were fashioned by hand, and loads were carried on sturdy backs. There were no beasts of burden and no practical use of the wheel (for transport, pottery making, or spinning threads). The high productivity levels of the Aztec economy derived from large, motivated, skilled, and well-organized labor forces.

A person's labor obligations were first and foremost committed to domestic sustenance and well-being. But there were many larger societal projects that put further demands on individuals. These projects occurred at *calpolli*, *altepetl*, and imperial levels. Every *calpolli* had a temple that needed to be maintained and occasionally renovated; at least some of this work was the responsibility of temple acolytes and lay assistants (Berdan, 2014: 234–235). Any noble's palace situated in a *calpolli* could also command local labor for everyday duties such as grinding maize, delivering firewood, supplying foodstuffs, or repairing and perhaps expanding the building itself (Hodge, 1991). Rulers and nobles also engaged artisans whose output was directed to their palaces (Hirth, 2016: 42–48). City-state rulers commanded similar types of labor from their residents for their everyday support. Since rulers' statuses were exalted, their palaces grandiose, and their households huge, provisioning required a substantial and constant investment of commoner labor. And not just palaces, but *altepetl* also relied on corvée labor (*coatequitl*) for maintenance of temples and other public buildings as well as repairs on basic infrastructure such as waterworks, plazas, roads, or walls. These tasks were allocated by majordomos associated with a ruler's palace (Figure 9).

Labor was also provided by slaves who usually acquired that status through individual misfortune, bad life decisions, or crime. They more closely resembled indentured servants than slaves in the more conventional sense. While most labor was channeled through the institutional economy, slaves could be bought and sold in marketplaces. The business was sufficiently lucrative to support merchants who specialized in slaves, and some cities (such as Azcapotzalco) were well-known for their slave markets. For the most part, slaves were engaged in domestic tasks, occasionally rented out as porters in marketplaces, and only rarely worked in agricultural fields (Berdan and Smith, 2021: 126–144; Hirth, 2016: 25).

Labor was also mobilized on the super-*altepetl* level. *Tlatoque* who ruled city-states in addition to their own could call upon those city-states for extraordinary

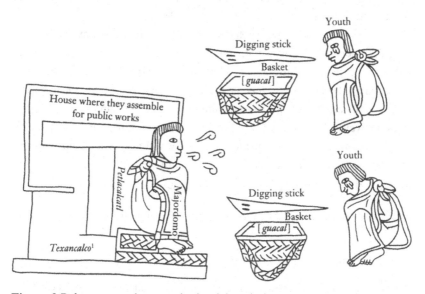

Figure 9 Palace mayordomo assigning labor duties. Berdan and Anawalt (1992, vol. 4: folio 70r).

labor needs. For instance, the cleanup of a flooded Tenochtitlan following Ahuitzotl's ill-fated aqueduct project was undertaken by a great many subject peoples: "the lords (and even those who were not lords) built as they wished because the construction was done by hands that were not theirs" (Durán, 1994: 372–373). When Motecuhzoma Xocoyotzin wished to move an enormous rock from Chalco to Tenochtitlan, he called on several neighboring city-states for the reported 10,000–12,000 laborers ultimately required (Alvarado Tezozomoc, 1975: 662). And the Mexica required their subject city-state of Cuitlahuac to "furnish maidens to dance in the feasts to the gods; from now on they would serve the Aztecs in their public works and in their personal service" (Durán, 1994: 121). These are just a few examples of the seemingly innumerable ways in which labor was controlled by and directed to the service of hierarchically based political entities. At the top, imperial rulers (*huey tlatoque* or "great rulers") could cast a wide net to secure laborers for scheduled or unforeseen projects.

Aztec city-states had no standing armies. Yet wars were frequent, forces were large, and warriors were well-trained. Commoner boys were instructed in military matters in their local *telpochcalli*, or "boys' school"; noble boys were similarly trained in the *calmecac*, which also offered a more erudite curriculum. All learned the culture of war from an early age: They heard of wars frequently and understood that their service could be required at any time. Ceremonies often reenacted conflicts. Men were motivated by prospects of prestige and material rewards from their own achievements and loot from a successful conquest. It was a labor force at the ready that opportunistically diverted men from their usual economic and other activities (Berdan and Smith, 2021: 208–231).

Land and labor were firmly rooted in the institutional economy. They were politically allocated and managed, and they provided economic support to the society's fundamental institutions (such as administrative palaces, temples, and the military). There were a few possible exceptions, such as documentary statements of occasionally purchased lands or slaves bought and sold in marketplaces. However, by and large, land and labor were not negotiated within the market economy; this does not mean that they were not entangled with the expanding commercial and market networks of the late Aztec world (see Section 5; Hicks, 1986: 50; Hirth, 2016: 36–48).

3.2 The Economics of Government: Palace, City-State, Empire, and Tribute

3.2.1 Palaces as Administrative Hubs for City-States (altepetl)

Every *altepetl* had its dynastic ruler, and every ruler had his urban palace. These palaces were the nerve centers of *altepetl* economic control and governmental administration. Opulent palaces embodied and furthered rulers' priorities of sustaining extraordinary lifestyles, promoting political ambitions, advancing wars, and maintaining favorable relations with the gods. Other nobles also enjoyed palatial lifestyles – the status, wealth, and power of rulers and nobles were proclaimed by the size and opulence of their palaces.

Royal palaces housed large polygynous households including the ruler, his many wives, multiple children, and a bevy of servants and slaves. The domestic palatial world consisted of warrens of living, eating, and sleeping rooms; sweatbaths; cooking facilities; and expansive gardens and courtyards. The king and his vast household also needed space for personal storage: the *conquistador* Andrés de Tapia (1963: 40) mentions that "Moctezuma had a house of many rooms and courtyards where he had robes and mantles and other things." And this was just clothing. Alva Ixtlilxochitl (1965: 266) enumerates some of the annual needs of the Texcocan royal palace under Nezahualpilli (r. 1472– 1515): 31,600 *fanegas* (a Spanish measure) of maize (1 *fanega* = 55.5 liters), 243 loads of cacao, 8,000 turkeys, 5,000 *fanegas* of chilis, 2,000 measures of salt, and 574,010 fine capes. This consumption most likely addresses the domestic arm of the palace.

Such palaces also served as city-states' administrative hubs – city-state governments were centered in royal palaces. As such, palaces contained vast rooms for government and its support. A brief tour around the administrative "wing" of the Texcocan ruler Nezahualcoyotl's (r. 1418–72) palace as outlined in the *Mapa Quinatzin* would reveal the royal dais facing a spacious courtyard; armories; meeting rooms for government officials, merchants, and warriors; rooms for visiting dignitaries; a music and arts room; and courtrooms (Douglas, 2010; Figure 10). This is surely just a sampling, since spaces for a granary, library, artisan workshops, aviary, zoo, observatory, and expansive gardens with clever water features are also mentioned for Tenochtitlan and other palaces (e.g., Cortés, 1928: 67–68; Evans, 2017; Sahagún, 1950–82, book 8). Activities in many of these spaces (such as courtrooms) were dedicated to city-state government. Since rulers and their city-states were inseparable, spaces such as zoos and gardens enhanced the reputation of a ruler and by extension the stature of his city-state. Additionally, imperial rulers also enjoyed pleasure palaces within and beyond their capital cities, all requiring high levels of staffing, supply, and maintenance (such as Huaxtepec in Morelos for Tenochtitlan's *huey tlatoani* and Texcotzinco for Texcoco's).

The ruler had expensive tastes and his government had diverse and recurring needs. Palatial storehouses needed to be stocked and constantly replenished. Most (if not all) day-to-day household support was supplied by commoners attached to or dependent on the palace (see Section 3.1.2). This included a great

Diagram of Nezahualcoyotl's Palace

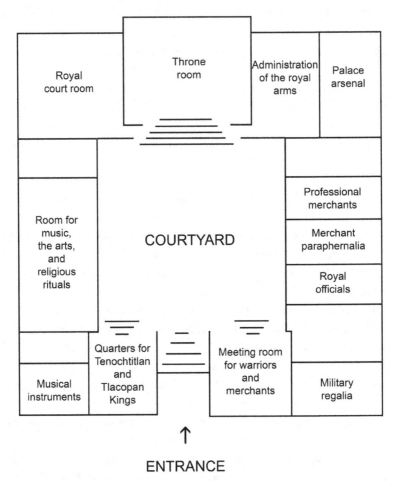

Figure 10 Nezahualcoyotl's palace. Drawing by Jennifer Berdan Lozano.

deal of food, firewood, charcoal, pottery, mats and baskets, clothing, and cacao beans delivered daily, weekly, biweekly, semiannually, or annually. For food, maize, chilis, tomatoes, turkeys, and salt are most often mentioned; the inevitable cacao beans were probably traded in markets for additional foods such as other grains, seasonal fruits and vegetables, and aquatic and avian fauna (Hicks, 1984; Hodge, 1991). Household labor was augmented by harnessing commoners within the palace's thrall: women to grind maize and men to do household chores such as sweeping floors, hauling water, and general palace maintenance (Hodge, 1991; Torquemada, 1969, vol. 1: 167). The Texcoco royal palace received these services on a rotating basis from the many towns in its domain (Hicks, 1984).

There were fine lines between regular household maintenance, the ruler's political persona, and administrative operations. Some of the foods supplied by commoners may well have been directed to the *tlatoani*'s feasts, events that unnerved enemies and solidified political alliances. Some goods were luxuries (such as greenstones and feathers delivered to the Teotihuacan *tlatoani*) and could have been transformed by palace artisans into fine adornments or given directly as political gifts. Weaponry given to that same *tlatoani* bolstered his armory in a conflict-laden environment (Hodge, 1991: 121, 125). Work undertaken by attached palace artisans, whether carpenters or feather workers, enhanced the appearance of the palace and proclaimed the wealth of its owner. Some goods were redistributed or regifted, these acts often reinforcing social and political hierarchies. For instance, in Cuauhtitlan around 1420, the ruler distributed undesignated tribute annually, probably to nobles to assure their loyalty. In 1548, a Xochimilco *tlatoani* received 240 canoes annually from his subjects; he kept one-third for himself, gave one-third to important nobles, and gave one-third to the *calpolli* people who worked his *chinampa* lands. These were gifts but also investments. This latter example is colonial but very likely reflects pre-Spanish patterns (Hodge, 1991: 124, 127).

These resource movements were fundamentally unidirectional; most goods and services were produced by commoners and consumed by the palace and its inhabitants for daily sustenance and political ends. Still, since generosity was a cultural virtue, some redistribution did occur. In these arrangements, commoners were tied to nobles at all levels (including rulers), lesser nobles were tied to higher nobles, higher nobles to city-state rulers, and on up to the political apex, the imperial *huey tlatoque*.

3.2.2 Imperial Strategies

A mere ninety-one years passed between the formation of the Triple Alliance in 1430 and the Spanish conquest in 1521. During that brief time span, the Aztec imperial powers pursued unrelenting conquests to politically control other city-state polities; extract economic resources, products, and finished goods from those city-states; and safeguard wide-ranging trade routes. This Aztec empire was formed as a coalition of three important Basin of Mexico city-states: Tenochtitlan, Texcoco, and Tlacopan. The rulers (*tlatoque*) of each of these city-states already controlled their own sources of royal revenue from earlier conquests; they were, in essence, "conquest states" (Smith, 1994: 315). Nearby in Morelos "most of the region's seventy city-states were subjugated by six conquest states that extracted tribute payments from their subjects" (Berdan, 2014: 138). Conquest of these states by the Triple Alliance yielded a political hierarchy whereby the least powerful city-states were attached to more powerful ones that in turn were embraced by the empire. Tribute and other obligations climbed the ladder accordingly.

The Triple Alliance powers also gained subjects and extracted tribute from collective conquests. Michael Smith and I (Berdan and Smith, 1996) have suggested that the Triple Alliance powers employed four primary strategies in building and integrating their empire: political, economic, elite, and frontier. All of these strategies incorporated economic dimensions and were differentially implemented throughout the empire's brief history.

The political strategy was pursued predominately within the Basin of Mexico where city-states were conquered early in the empire's history and hands-on political control was feasible. This strategy involved the greatest amount of meddling exercised by the empire. In some cases, the rulers of conquered city-states were replaced by imperial relatives; in others, conquered city-states lost their local *tlatoani* office entirely with the new government managed by an installed governor. Either way, the imperial powers tightened their control over these nearby polities by guaranteeing loyalty and compliance through kinship, offers of political boons, and economic reciprocities. The Triple Alliance rulers could confidently count on established tribute payments and occasional labor demands from these polities. The imperial rulers frequently called upon these city-states in their distant military expeditions. In so doing, the imperial powers gained essential manpower while the subject city-states and their warriors potentially gained political favor, social status, shares of conquest booty, and material and symbolic rewards (Figure 11).

The economic strategy was based on military conquest of city-states both within and beyond the Basin of Mexico. These conquests yielded immediate loot as well as long-term, regular tribute payments paid by thirty-eight "tributary provinces" based on the *Codex Mendoza* tribute tally (see Section 3.2.3). Beyond the Basin of Mexico, most vanquished city-states were allowed to retain their dynastic rulers in their traditional positions and were largely left alone as long as they continued to pay their negotiated tributes and did not openly rebel. The installation of Aztec governors and/or military garrisons did occur but not as a matter of course. Conquered city-states were expected to provide provisions and sometimes warriors to Aztec armies marching through their territories on their way to more distant wars. They were also expected to attend state events in the Triple Alliance capitals; refusal was tantamount to an act of rebellion. The economic strategy also encompassed political promotion of

Figure 11 A warrior earns rewards of regalia and decorated cape. Berdan and Anawalt (1992, vol. 4: folio 64r).

long-distance trade. Some professional merchants (*pochteca*) were sponsored by Basin of Mexico city-state rulers to carry their royal goods on combined diplomatic/commercial expeditions. Rulers also dabbled in the workings of the intricate market system, drawing income from market taxes within the Basin of Mexico and, in one documented case, requiring the availability of specific goods at the distant market of Tepeacac (Berdan and Smith, 1996: 210; Durán, 1994: 159).

The elite strategy had ancient roots in Mesoamerica, long predating the ascendency of the Aztecs. It involved the forging of close ties between city-states at high social and political levels, primarily through marriages. The Aztecs practiced elite polygyny, which gave rulers and other powerful nobles ample opportunity to establish political alliances through carefully crafted marriages. It was common practice for a higher-ranking (e.g., imperial) ruler to offer a daughter in marriage to a subordinate ruler. This reaffirmed the dominant/subordinate relations between the rulers and assured next-generation loyalties (as the children of this marriage would claim Aztec as well as local legitimacy). Over time, a complex tangle of royal relatives developed, sometimes resulting in ambiguous and conflicting loyalties among city-state rulers. Elite marriages carried with them obligatory gift exchanges, including land and its associated laborers along with the most exquisite finery available. Political alliances were also forged and cemented through feasting, requiring massive outlays of food, flowers, and tobacco along with gifts such as weapons, ornate clothing, and fancy adornments. In addition, as the empire matured, some conquered elites in outlying regions added Nahuatl to their linguistic repertoires, facilitating political communications and further integrating subject elites into the imperial web.

Wars were expensive. The frontier strategy provided an alternative way to control outlying regions by establishing client states primarily along perpetually hostile borderlands and astride precarious trade routes. Client states (see Luttwak, 1976) were brought into the imperial orbit through negotiation or military intimidation. Instead of paying regularly scheduled tributes, these city-states offered gifts to the imperial powers, receiving gifts in return. Both sides benefited from these arrangements. Along hostile borderlands, client states provided buffer zones protecting tribute-paying city-states, prohibited large states such as the Tarascans and Tlaxcallans from encroaching on Aztec territory, and allowed the empire to commit its military energies and resources elsewhere. Along trade routes, client states assured the safety of merchants and their goods to and from the imperial capitals. For their part, client states received support in the form of weaponry and defenses in their own borderland wars, all the while enjoying the "aura" of imperial power at their back. They gave "gifts" at irregular intervals (from battlefield captives to clothing to gold) rather than the more onerous tribute. In general, this strategy was effective and inexpensive in holding restless borderlands and protecting vulnerable merchants.

Forceful and opportunistic as these strategies were, they did not always work. The aforementioned Tarascans served up a disastrous defeat to the imperial armies under Axayacatl in 1478. The Tlaxcallans and Huexotzincas to the east were persistent Aztec enemies; furious and determined battles with them were frequent. The armies fought to stalemates. Although these are described as ritualized "flower wars" fought for practice and honor, they appear to have been fought completely in earnest with the Aztec powers fully intent on conquest (Berdan, 2014: 158). Other unconquered city-states dotted the central Mexican landscape, resulting in a geographically discontinuous domain. By 1519, the empire's continued expansion was largely blocked by stubborn powerful polities (and both oceans), and expansionist wars of the second Motecuhzoma (r. 1502–20) were interrupted by frequent rebellions. Unsuccessful wars and sometimes unanswered rebellions drained that ruler's coffers and did nothing to augment them.

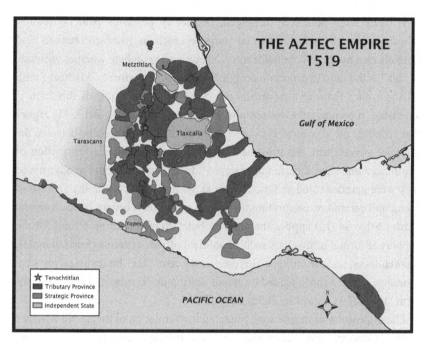

Figure 12 The Aztec empire, 1519. Drawing by Jennifer Berdan Lozano.

A constructed map of 1519 central Mexico shows city-states incorporated into the Aztec empire through two of these main strategies: economic and frontier (Figure 12). The economic strategy yielded "tributary provinces," groupings of historically and/or geographically related city-states, although often loosely so. The frontier strategy produced "strategic provinces," clusters of similarly related city-states. "Provinces" appear to be more of a top-down administrative convenience rather than a natural clustering of nearby city-states (Berdan, 2014: 171–173). The seventeen strategic provinces largely provided borderland and trade route protections, but the thirty-eight tributary provinces were the economic mainstay of the empire with their vast tribute deliveries (Berdan, 1996: 135).

3.2.3 Imperial Tribute and Taxes

Tribute was quintessential political economy. Terms of payments were negotiated as the final act of military conquests and tributes thereafter ceremonially delivered to the imperial overlords on regular schedules. Raw materials and finished goods moved one-way, from conquered subjects to the coffers of imperial rulers to be used in support of social, political, and religious institutions. Vanquished city-states saw little in return other than potential aid in habitual conflicts with their own hostile neighbors.

Tributes were politically arranged, obligatory demands paid on regular schedules or delivered for special purposes such as royal coronations and funerals or a major temple dedication. There is some debate whether "tribute" or "tax" is the most appropriate designation for these payments. Michael Smith (2015) argues that these payments represent "taxes" and use of this term is amenable to comparative discussions. Berdan (Berdan et al., 2017: 11) argues that "tribute" more accurately "conveys the political relationships between the imperial government and subjects . . . as well as the symbolic affirmation of dominance and subordination they signal." Indeed, when tribute goods arrived they were paraded through Tenochtitlan to the royal palace with the greatest of pomp and ceremony, celebrating the ruler's power over distant lands. Kenneth Hirth (2016: 34–35) applies the term "tribute" to resources mobilized for the support of formal institutions such as political offices, palaces, courts, temples, marketplaces, and the military. He reserves the term "tax" for levies on physical products, such as those placed on goods sold in marketplaces. Here, I use the term "tribute" as argued by Berdan and Hirth.

The imposition of tribute long predated the formation of the Triple Alliance empire. Conquest states came and went, with tribute an expectation and reality of conquest. The Mexica themselves paid tribute in labor, goods, and military service to the powerful Tepaneca of Azcapotzalco for much of the fourteenth century. So, the Triple Alliance powers were continuing a timeworn tradition when they imposed tribute on their conquered subjects. They did not invent tribute, but they did expand it to a level hitherto unknown in Mesoamerican civilizations.

Imperial tribute payments are mentioned in numerous documents but are especially detailed in two codices, the *Matrícula de Tributos* and part two of the *Codex Mendoza* (Figure 13). The former is very likely a pre-Spanish codex, while the latter, perhaps a copy of the *Matrícula*, was composed twenty years after the Spanish conquest. The two exhibit few differences: the *Mendoza* lists thirty-eight provinces, while the *Matrícula* lists thirty-three (due to missing pages), and there are patterned variances in format, style, and quantities of goods. A similar textual document, the *Información de 1554*, encompasses most of the same provinces but lists somewhat different items and quantities (Berdan, 1992a).

According to the *Codex Mendoza*, clothing and other textiles, staple foodstuffs (maize, beans, chia, and amaranth), and feathered warrior costumes were the most common tribute items, delivered by thirty-six, twenty, and twenty-nine provinces, respectively. Other foods consisted of chilis, honey, cacao, and salt. Utilitarian goods included reed mats, woods and firewood, lime, carrying frames, and pottery bowls. Distant provinces delivered luxurious raw materials

(52

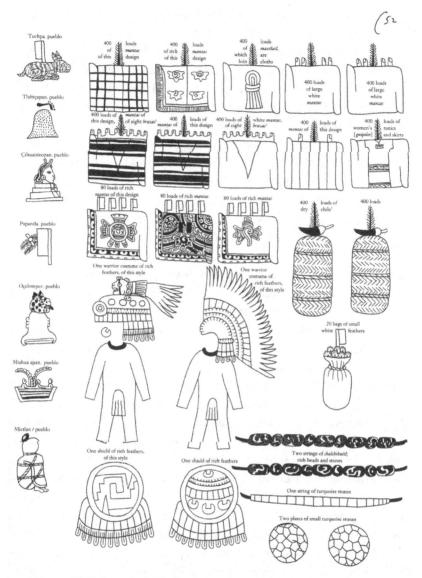

Figure 13 Tribute from Tochpan province. Berdan and Anawalt (1992, vol. 4: folio 52r).

and manufactured goods such as turquoise mosaics, strings of finished greenstones, colorful feathers, gold adornments, fine lip plugs, and jaguar pelts in their tribute payments. A comprehensive list of tributes paid to the empire can be found in Berdan (1992b).

It is likely that the *Matrícula* and *Mendoza* were not complete records of tribute assessments and that they registered tributes for a single point in time (probably between 1516 and 1518 for the *Matrícula*; see Berdan, 1992a). Diego Durán (1994: 202–207) provides a long and detailed list of tributes, mentioning goods such as marine fauna, live snakes, bees in their hives, weapons and cotton armor, and a variety of fruits and flowers, above and beyond those goods contained in the abovementioned tribute tallies. Indeed, Durán (1994: 206, 358) insists that tribute consisted of "all things created under the sky" and was so rich and diverse that "it exceeds the imagination, is impossible to describe." Additional documentary sources mention even more diverse tributes for city-states under the imperial umbrella: turkeys, wild game, fine woods for carving, live deer, obsidian blades, fish, shellfish, and even alligator teeth (Berdan, 1996: 127–129).

Imperial tributes were paid on annual, semiannual, or eighty-day (or quarterly) schedules in the *Matrícula de Tributos/Codex Mendoza* tallies. Staple foodstuffs and warrior costumes were delivered annually, being weighty and awkward in transport. Some luxury goods, required of distant provinces, were also usually paid annually (far-distant Xoconochco is an exception, paying everything twice a year). Whatever the payment schedule, deliveries were typically made in the same calendrical months: Tlacaxipehualiztli, Etzalcualiztli, Ochpaniztli, and Panquetzaliztli. These concentrated arrivals of exorbitant tribute materially punctuated the extraordinary power of the imperial rulers.

Tributes were paid by provinces near and far and were therefore subject to transport and cost–distance considerations. All conveyance took place with the aid of tumplines and pack frames or containers on the backs of porters (*tlameme*) or in canoes (see Hassig, 1985). Canoe transport was far more efficient than human carriers but limited to the availability of lake or riverine systems (most notably in the Basin of Mexico). Common estimates for individual *tlameme* loads range from 23 to 30 kg (51 to 66 pounds), although Hirth (2016: 240) argues convincingly for heavier loads. In terms of commodities, 20 cotton cloaks constituted 1 porter's load (*carga*), and 24,000 cacao beans equaled 1 *carga*. Demands on porters would vary depending on practical matters such as the nature of the terrain, weather conditions, planned daily distances, overall length of the journey, and number of porters available. Flexibility was key.

Given these transport constraints, it is not surprising that most heavy and bulky goods were obtained from nearby subjects, while less weighty materials and goods were derived from more distant provinces. Staple foodstuffs, for instance, were delivered almost exclusively from provinces in and around the Basin of Mexico with only two exceptions, Tepeacac to the east and Coyolapan in the Valley of Oaxaca. It is possible that Coyolapan's tribute foodstuffs did not actually travel to Tenochtitlan but were stored locally to support an imposed Aztec garrison and two governors, as well as armies and state-sponsored merchants in their treks through these lands. Tepeacac also supported Aztec installations and administrators (Berdan and Anawalt, 1992, vol. 2: 99, 107; Mohar Betancourt, 2013: 59; Smith and Berdan, 1996: 281, 285). In general, conquered populations were required to supply food, weapons, and military aid to whatever administrative officers or military garrisons the Aztecs installed in their lands. Even considering the possible anomalies of Tepeacac and Coyolapan, cost–distance factors seem to have played a significant role in assessments, since maize, beans, and other staples were produced in virtually every nook and cranny of the empire. Cacao, grown in lowland regions, presented transport challenges as well. Janine Gasco estimates that cacao tribute carried from the most distant province (Xoconochco) amounted to 2.5 metric tons twice a year – "a daunting physical and logistical effort" (Berdan, 2014: 164–165). Weight and bulk were not the only considerations; transport difficulties appeared in other guises. For instance, moving with live deer required more than tumplines, and the transport of live bees and their hives must have been a bit tricky. The conveyance of live sea corals in heavy water containers – from the Gulf Coast to Tenochtitlan, a journey of 250 kilometers over rough terrain – must have been a particularly unwieldy and cumbersome undertaking (Medina-Rosas et al., 2021).

Tribute demands were largely based on local resource availabilities and reflected local ecologies. But this does not mean that all tribute products and goods were locally produced; some clearly needed to be acquired by trade or other means from neighboring or distant areas (see Section 5.2.3). These interactions were economically important: The imposition of tribute reinforced and stimulated trade throughout the empire and beyond and allowed the Triple Alliance access to goods beyond its actual imperial borders. Additionally, tribute levies often included manufactured goods, encouraging specialized production in conquered provinces.

The most prevalent imperial officials in conquered provinces were tribute collectors or *calpixque* (sing. *calpixqui*). They either resided in the provinces or were periodically sent there from the imperial capitals. Understandably, they were not popular among the local people, whether nobles or commoners. There were different styles of tribute collection in the provinces. In one scenario, nearby communities presented their tributes to their provincial city-state capital where *calpixque* assembled the goods for delivery to the imperial overlords. Alternatively, *calpixque* traveled from community to community in a more hands-on collection approach. In either case, provincial subjects most likely supplied the porters to transport the loads. It is possible that processes of local tribute collection involved negotiation and exchange of specific goods, as suggested for the province of Tlapa in present-day Guerrero (Gutiérrez, 2013). Once delivered to the imperial capitals, tribute goods were deposited and secured in storehouses supervised by a *petlacalcatl*, or tribute overseer. Documents suggest that, at the imperial level, tributes may well have been delivered first to Tenochtitlan and then divided among the three allies, with two-fifths to Tenochtitlan, two-fifths to Texcoco, and one-fifth to the less powerful Tlacopan (Berdan, 1992a: 63–64). This is a generalized portrayal; the entire tribute collection system was probably more multilayered, bureaucratic, and varied (Durán, 1971: 201; Smith, 2015: 95–101).

Tributes substantially increased the wealth and material security of the imperial rulers, their palatial households, and their governmental bureaucracies. Tributes also enhanced imperial political and military power and contributed both materially and symbolically to future alliances and conquests. Some weaponry from tributes augmented the ruler's armory. Conquering rulers rewarded their bravest warriors with decorated cloaks and special feathered regalia, the latter worn in battle and inspiring their fellow warriors to courageous feats. Alliance was a complement to war, and the imperial rulers invited powerful political friends and foes to lavish banquets with the intent of forging alliances with some or controlling others through intimidation. At these feasts, royal hosts must be exquisitely adorned, and their gifts to guests must be beyond luxurious. Imperial rulers found a good selection for themselves and guests in their tribute storehouses. Palace artisans were supplied from royal storehouses with raw materials for their masterpieces, and professional merchants commissioned by rulers carried goods (given in tribute) on pack frames (also given in tribute) to distant trading centers (see Section 5.3.2). Tributes contributed broadly to palace and government: Live eagles were brought to royal zoos, jaguar skins were draped on the royal seat, and paper was stacked for codex making. Cacao and large white cotton cloaks (*quachtli*) could be exchanged in markets for other necessities.

Rulers were expected to be generous, and tribute stores provided the means by which they could support widows and orphans and distribute food to their populace at specified ceremonies. Rulers also routinely compensated artisans, construction workers, bureaucratic officials, and traveling merchants with goods ranging from cloaks and cacao to foods and pottery. Foodstuffs paid in tribute bolstered the food supply in the imperial cities (especially the extraordinarily large Tenochtitlan), and substantial stores of food provided at least temporary respite in times of famine. Beyond these practical uses and investments, tribute served as a symbolic statement reinforcing political and military supremacy over vast domains.

Tribute also contributed to financing the society's vast religious infrastructure, diverse ritual paraphernalia, and flamboyant ceremonies that punctuated Aztec daily life.

3.3 Religious Financing

Politics and religion were inseparable in Aztec life. Major temples were located close to royal palaces in city-state centers, and rulers played essential roles in constructing temples and performing religious ceremonies. Palace artisans, drawing on tribute stores, fashioned splendid adornments for deities housed in temple shrines. Tributes from the *tlatoque*'s coffers supplied at least some of the paraphernalia used for daily priestly support and rituals as well as the more flamboyant calendric ceremonies. Some religious ceremonies carried political overtones, their extravagance a signal of power and intimidation to invited political visitors.

Religion in Aztec times was not only intense and theatrical; it was also expensive. Religious infrastructure and performance required a great deal of material outlay, which was variously obtained from rulers and their treasuries, temple neophytes, ceremonial participants, and efforts of the priests and priestesses themselves.

Every city-state gave pride of place to religious structures and activities. Depending on the size and importance of the city-state, central ceremonial precincts would contain one or more temples (*teocalli*), priestly quarters and oratories, temple schools for noble boys (*calmecac*), ball courts, skull racks (*tzompantli*), sacrificial stones, and various ritual platforms and monoliths. The sacred precinct of Tenochtitlan, for example, contained all of these as well as armories, warriors' assembly rooms, housing for foreign dignitaries, and replicas of sacred landscapes such as springs and a "small arid environment" (López Luján, 2020: 173). These precincts were not only imposing; they were also extensive. For priestly lodgings alone, Cortés (1928: 89, 90) speaks of "sumptuous lodgings" in buildings with "large halls and corridors." Tenochtitlan's sacred precinct was undoubtedly oversized, in keeping with that city's extraordinary population size (200,000–250,000). Other less imposing temple precincts were situated in the city's districts. But no matter how small, each city-state featured its own ceremonial center, always with a major temple and often with a selection of these other structures. All of this religious infrastructure needed to be constructed, embellished, maintained, and repaired when needed.

Temples were big-ticket items and most realistically financed by *tlatoque*. The more resources rulers put in to building major temples, the greater the visual acclaim to their own power and their demonstrated dedication to the gods. Construction was labor-intensive and drew on a *tlatoani*'s ability to harness large workforces and abundant materials. For example, Tenochtitlan's Templo Mayor was completely expanded seven times (and it and its environs were partially extended or refurbished several more times) between 1325 and

1520. For one of these projects, the first Motecuhzoma (r. 1440–68) requested that four allied and subject city-states (Texcoco, Tlacopan, Chalco, and Xochimilco) each construct a side of the temple, contributing not just labor but also materials. They complied. Even more workers may have been involved; it was a project of some urgency such that "people from all the provinces worked like ants in the construction" (Durán, 1994: 225–227). The completion of another of these expansions, in 1487, was celebrated with extraordinary ceremonial and political ostentation. In addition to human sacrificial ceremonies, the delivery of tributes from near and far was featured: vast amounts of gold, precious feathers and stones, clothing and adornments, cacao, and all manner of foods. These goods were managed by the royal treasurer, and "Especially everything the priests requested for the cult to the gods and for the present ceremonies was provided" (Durán, 1994: 336). These were impositions made by a ruler but for primarily religious purposes (although, admittedly, the *tlatoani* himself reaped rewards of power, stature, and godly favor).

Other religious structures and monuments also relied on economic support from polity and populace. Massive sacrificial stones and other monoliths required huge labor investments in moving the rocks into the city centers, efforts only available to powerful *tlatoque* (see Section 3.1.2 and Berdan, 2014: 149–150). Murals decorated walls, stone monoliths were transformed into sacred sculptures by skilled artisans, and godly idols housed in temple shrines were divinely adorned with cloth, gold, shells, feathers, and fine stone artistry. Some idols themselves were made from wood or stone, but others were fashioned from amaranth dough. Other materials used in religious infrastructure and accoutrements included woods, lime, paints, reeds, obsidian mirrors, and flowers.

Some of these materials likely were provided by rulers from their tribute coffers. Construction materials were paid in tribute and also provided by designated city-states for specific projects (see Section 3.2.3). Godly garments were woven and embroidered by priestesses in temples, possibly using cotton paid in tribute to the local ruler and donated to the temple. Copal was used as incense and copious quantities were given in tribute, as was amaranth. Gold, feathers, and precious stone adornments were produced by palace artisans, at least in Tenochtitlan, and all of these materials appear on the *Codex Mendoza* tribute tally (Sahagún, 1950–82, book 8: 91). Other daily needs were provided by neophyte priests: collecting maguey spines, firewood, and fir branches; maintaining fires; offering incense; and making temple repairs. Some temples and their idols were cared for by the local faithful, especially occupational groups dedicated to a patron deity (Berdan, 2007: 255). Some individuals dedicated themselves to temple service for one year (performing guarding and sweeping duties), in exchange for future good fortune. Youths at the Templo Mayor decorated the temple, served the resident priests, cared for obsidian blades, and did general manual work. Young women cooked food for the idol and probably also for the priests. Since deities were many and each deity had his or her own temple, this lay support must have been considerable across the land. It was also inexpensive. Youths at the Templo Mayor, for instance, were "on their own" for their daily sustenance, begging for alms or picking off the odd ear of maize from fields.

Temples had "keepers" (*teohua*) who were responsible for procuring needed materials and items for ongoing temple maintenance and functioning (Sahagún, 1950–82, book 2: 206–215). Perhaps it was they who appealed to the palace's tribute overseers; surely they or their underlings scoured the marketplaces for daily necessities.

The needs of priests, from their daily fare to their specialized garments and ritual paraphernalia, were met by tributes, temple offerings and gifts, alms, volunteered or conscripted labor, yields from the rather enigmatic temple lands (*teopantlalli*), and even ritualized stealing (Berdan, 2007: 256). Beyond these, some priests went to war where they potentially garnered social status and economic gain by capturing enemy warriors. They were rewarded with regalia and cloaks, some likely from their ruler's tribute stores (Berdan and Anawalt, 1992, vol. 3: folio 65r). Durán (1994: 204) describes a white dress worn by temple women that was given in tribute. Much other ritual paraphernalia (such as priestly tunics, incense burners, black paint, priestly bags, tobacco pouches, banners, and sacrificial knives) do not appear on the *Codex Mendoza* tribute tally. Perhaps they were included in Durán's more inclusive list of "all things created under the sky," or priests obtained them through gifts and offerings, marketplace exchanges, or in-temple production (Figure 14).

Most religious ceremonies were scheduled and repetitive, conforming to the well-known calendrical system (Figure 15). Other ceremonial events were less predictable: a ruler's coronation or funeral, the dedication of a temple, or the return of victorious troops. Both types were religious or religious/political hybrids, were extravagant, and required substantial material outlays. As with temples and priests, ceremonial success relied on support from both ruler and populace.

Most of the eighteen monthly ceremonies combined household and public rituals, people contributing to their in-house celebrations (with, especially, foods and flowers) and participating and making offerings in the public sphere. The economic burden of serving the gods ceremonially was distributed broadly throughout the population. At some point in the year, men and women, young and old, ruler and farmer, merchant and warrior, mat maker and midwife, and

Figure 14 Priest with incense burner. Berdan and Anawalt (1992, vol. 4: folio 63r).

Figure 15 Religious procession. Nuttall (1903, folio 35).

more, all enjoyed opportunities to publicly celebrate and demonstrate their dedication to the gods and their community. For at least some events, the degree of participation was basically prorated by the ability to pay: Wealthy nobles were expected to contribute more; poor farmers offered what they could. A common theme in these ceremonies is reciprocity, from exchanges of food in households to transactions between people and the deities: "economic commitments and investments were made by everyone in the society, no matter their station in life. Every person had a stake in and responsibility toward these life-ensuring events" (Berdan, 2017: 153).

Regularly scheduled ceremonies also impacted marketplaces. Each religious event required its special materials and paraphernalia, and occupational specialists would gear up production prior to each ceremony to meet heightened consumer demand. These spikes in demand notably affected pottery makers, carpenters, paper makers, spinners and weavers, reed workers, and feather workers, all selling their products in marketplaces.

Religious ceremonies frequently required offerings. The ritual offerings in Tenochtitlan's ceremonial precinct collectively contain thousands upon thousands of materials, animal and human remains, and artifacts (López Luján, 2005). The vast majority of deposited items came from beyond the Basin of Mexico. It is reasonable to look to tribute as a logical source of these materials, but "Relatively few of the tribute goods [listed in the *Codex Mendoza*] ... were destined for the state cult, especially those delivered to the priests to be buried as offerings" (López Luján, 2019: 29). Alternatively, these materials and goods could have reached the hands of priests through special-purpose tribute collections, long-distance trade, or exchanges in marketplaces. Some of the trade itself was staggering: Live sea corals whose transport necessitated large water tanks came from as far away as today's Baja California, 1,300 kilometers distant (Medina-Rosas et al., 2021: 27).

4 Specialization

Specialization is generally considered as "a differentiated, regularized, permanent, and perhaps institutionalized production system in which producers depend on extra-household exchange relationships at least in part for their livelihood, and consumers depend on them for acquisition of goods they do not produce themselves" (Costin, 1991: 4). This definition pertains to the production of physical goods, and in these terms, the Aztec world was full of specialists. These included agricultural and nonagricultural food producers and a multitude of craftspeople from potters to sandal makers to lapidaries. Women were exclusive producers of spun thread and woven cloth. But other economic, political, and religious specialization occurred at all levels and in every corner of this complex society. There were merchants on many scales who entered the economic world as intermediaries in commodity chains, service providers (such as porters, barbers, midwives, scribes, and teachers), and power specialists such as government bureaucrats, high-ranking warriors, and cadres of priests. While not producing goods, they fulfilled societal needs as specialists, in turn relying on others for goods and services.

The Aztecs drew on a long history of specialization in Mesoamerica, reaching back millennia (Manzanilla, 2006). In Aztec times, specialization was especially made possible through intensive agricultural systems (see Section 2): Agricultural and nonagricultural production created storable surpluses that allowed some persons to be released from food-producing pursuits. The population surge at this time also contributed to specialization, providing increasing numbers and concentrations of both producers and consumers. The expanding commercialization of the Aztec economy also stimulated and facilitated specialization (see Section 5).

Throughout the Aztec world, specialization was found in a variety of contexts and on many different scales; it also operated under differing degrees of social and political constraints. Some specialists were attached to royal and noble palaces, others operated more independently; some worked full-time at their specialty, others were part-time specialists; some worked voluntarily, others (such as slaves), involuntarily. Specialists, in whatever arena, could focus their time and attention on singular activities, affording opportunities for innovation as well as enhanced quality and quantity, thereby stimulating the production of surpluses. But specialization also entailed risks. A potter needed to calculate shifting demands for his product, as well as competition from the new potter next door. A merchant worried about the availability of sufficient porters for his next long trek. A canoe maker pondered the dwindling number of trees for his craft. Things were complicated for feather workers, who needed a wide array of materials at hand, all at the same time. Midwives needed to constantly reinforce their reputations, and government bureaucrats needed to maintain political favor. Breakdowns in any of these (and so many more) situations highlight the precariousness of specialized occupations and the possibly limited alternatives to people should they fail. On the positive side, these many anxieties were mitigated by the highly dynamic character of Aztec life: The population was surging, the economy was growing, and the empire was expanding.

Understanding Aztec specialization would be a bit unwieldy were it not for Cathy Costin's (1991) multifaceted model that considers dimensions of context, concentration, scale, and intensity. Although she analyzes craft production in particular, her dimensions are useful in understanding any specialization.

Context refers to the organizational milieu of the specialist and the type and extent of control over that specialist's activities. We have already seen, in Section 2, that a great deal of craft production took place in individual households. Those pursuits were often combined with other household activities and undertaken intermittently during convenient times of the year. Some of these households were attached to or sponsored by royal or noble palaces; others worked more independently. Sometimes the context is unclear: Were stone workers who carved Motecuhzoma Xocoyotzin's likeness on a stone in Chapultepec attached to the royal palace or were they independent artisans? Either way, they were paid handsomely by that ruler: Each received a slave, and they divided among themselves loads of maize, beans, chilis, cacao, and men's and women's clothing (Durán, 1994: 481).

An example of the contrasting advantages and risks of working in each of these contexts is afforded by the feather workers who are also discussed in Section 2.2. Feather-work artisans worked either independently in *calpolli* settings or attached to royal or noble palaces. If independent, they obtained their many materials and tools from merchants or other marketplace vendors; if attached, they had access to markets and merchants but especially to their sponsor's on-site aviary and palace stores, typically stocked by tribute payments. Palace feather workers worked in close proximity to fellow artisans: painters/scribes, goldsmiths, stone cutters, stone mosaic workers, and wood carvers (all of which, conveniently, contributed to the production of actual feathered objects). In the Tenochtitlan royal palace, they were responsible for the feathered attire and adornments of the god Huitzilopochtli and the ruler himself. They probably also fashioned the exquisite gifts given to visiting rulers and dignitaries. Independent feather workers sold their finished objects, including warrior regalia, in marketplaces. In these two different settings, feather workers made somewhat different objects but used the same techniques and followed the same procedures. And whether in *calpolli* or palace, they adhered to the same allocation and coordination of labor (see Section 2.2). While the documents do not directly say so, I believe that individual and complete feather-working households worked at (or for) their palace sponsors; a ruler or noble did not engage simply a feather worker but rather his entire household with its well-honed internal division of labor. In either setting, shortages in materials and imbalances in labor availability could be offset by neighboring colleagues. Palace feather workers enjoyed advantages of materials availability, proximity to allied artisans, and an established and known consumer. Their risks were relatively low, but they would have been required to produce objects according to fairly strict canons: Huitzilopochtli's array must be symbolically precise, political gifts must overwhelm the recipients, and the ruler's dancing costume must look just so. There was relatively little room for creativity in such a setting. Conversely, the independent feather worker probably had more artistic license but suffered

Figure 16 Turquoise mosaic. Courtesy National Museum of the American Indian, Smithsonian Institution, no. 108708.

greater anxieties over access to materials (through less predictable merchants and markets) and the vagaries of consumer demand.

This is just one specialization. It is particularly well-documented, and others, such as turquoise mosaic making, likely followed similar patterns (Figure 16). But what about non-craft specialists? In what kind of context did they make a living? Expansive palaces required many workers with specialized training. For instance, the creatures in Motecuhzoma Xocoyotzin's aviary and zoo were tended by hundreds of knowledgeable persons, and the specialized attention paid to intricate palatial gardens should not be underestimated. We do not know if such attached persons lived on-site or maintained households elsewhere. Some independent specialists, including professional merchants, were clustered in *calpolli* and enjoyed the support of their neighboring colleagues. Priests appear to have lived in priestly quarters at temples, but we do not know if their scribe and teacher associates also lived there or in separate households outside the sacred precinct. As in many other arenas of Aztec life, it is likely that there was a great deal of flexibility in how people maneuvered about in their work and living milieu.

Concentration covers the physical location of specialized activities – where people worked. This may refer to a household, various households (for a midwife, for example), *calpolli*, palace, or marketplace. Specialists could be

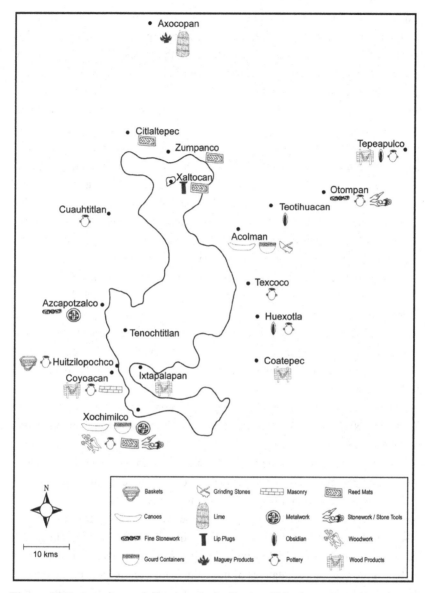

Figure 17 Economic specializations in the Basin of Mexico. Drawing by Jennifer Berdan Lozano.

concentrated in cities and countryside and in the imperial heartland as well as distant reaches of the Aztec empire (Figure 17).

Specializations abounded in the Basin of Mexico, the empire's core region. There, craft specialists were often situated near essential raw materials: Maguey-processing took place in maguey-growing areas in the northern Basin, wood workers were located in the forested piedmont, and mat makers and basket weavers near the lake. The concentration of obsidian working at Teotihuacan, Tepeapulco, and Otompan is not surprising, given the nearby sources of obsidian at Otompan and Pachuca. Paper making was a common specialization just south of the Basin of Mexico, where the *amaquahuitl* ("paper tree") grew in abundance (Smith, 2003: 253). Minc (2009) has shown that city-states producing ceramics made with specific clays were located close to their clay sources.

These raw material/production concurrences were convenient but not invariable. A great deal of cotton cloth was manufactured in highland regions where cotton could not be grown. Similarly, fine feathered regalia and garments were produced in the highlands although the colorful feathers essential to those crafts were not natively available in highland environments. Clearly, specializations could develop into thriving enterprises whether basic raw materials were locally available or not, the latter relying on dependable trade and market networks.

Some city-states became renowned for particular specializations. In the Basin of Mexico, Texcoco polychrome pottery was truly distinguished, Xochimilco lapidary work was prized, and Cuauhtitlan was the place to go for red jars. Azcapotzalco was renowned for silverwork, Coyoacan for masons and wood products, and other communities for basket weaving, mat making, maguey processing, carpentry, sculpting, and specific styles of pottery (Berdan, 2014: 107; Blanton, 1996; Blanton and Hodge, 1996). Both clothing and pottery exhibited recognizable *altepetl* and regional variations in form and designs (Hirth and Nichols, 2017: 289; Minc, 2017: 359). Some specializations were concentrated at the *calpolli* level; the *calpolli* of Amantlan in Tlatelolco became such a famous feather-working center that all feather workers came to be called *amanteca*. Specialists such as *pulque* makers, dyers, painters, gold workers, mat makers, stone workers, curers, and professional merchants were localized in specific Tenochtitlan–Tlatelolco *calpolli* (López Austin, 1973: 65–75; Monzon, 1949). In some cases, these concentrations and reputations derived from a city-state's proactive *tlatoani* in drawing specialists into his domain; this happened in Texcoco where representatives of more than thirty crafts were brought there by Texcoco's ruler and settled in their own districts (Alva Ixtlilxochitl, 1965, vol. 1: 326–327).

Some specialized production took place directly within marketplaces. This is well-documented for the fashioning of obsidian blades, perhaps "on order" (Anonymous Conqueror, 1963: 179; Díaz del Castillo, 2008: 174; Hirth, 2009c: 91). Marketplaces provided the setting for other specialists plying their trades, from barbers to porters to prostitutes. Other specialists, by the nature of their occupation, worked outside the household or palace. For instance, service providers such as midwives, curers, and diviners visited their clients; some tribute collectors traveled from community to community; and merchants likewise spent much of their time on the road. Some settings were limited or fixed: Zookeepers required a zoo, teachers a school, priests a temple, and tribute overseers a palace storehouse.

Ethnicity also played a part in spatial patterns of production. For instance, rod-shaped lip plugs that particularly signaled Otomí identity have been found archaeologically at Xaltocan, an Otomí community (Brumfiel, 1994). Perhaps less expected is the extent to which groups readily adopted other people's ethnic markers: Motecuhzoma Xocoyotzin enjoyed dining on Cholula polychrome pottery, the Aztec empire demanded ethnically designed clothing in tribute, and the empire required eighteen provinces to deliver ethnically styled Huaxteca regalia in tribute (although none of these were in Huaxteca territory) (Figure 18).

The empire's core had no monopoly on specialization; it proliferated throughout the imperial domain. Tribute paid to Aztec overlords included many types and considerable quantities of fully or partially manufactured

Figure 18 Huaxteca warrior costume. Berdan and Anawalt (1992, vol. 4: folio 64r).

goods: textiles (some elaborately decorated), feathered warrior costumes and shields, fine greenstone beads, turquoise mosaics, gold ornaments, lip plugs, copper bells and axes, bowls, smoking tubes, paper, and wooden carrying frames (Berdan and Anawalt, 1992, vol. 3). It can be argued that tribute impositions encouraged and stimulated economic production in subject city-states as they strove to fulfill the demands of their conquerors.

Scale considers the number of persons engaged in the specialization and the social relations among them. These are not easy to determine with the documentary and archaeological information at hand. But a few things are clear. Crafting and other specialized undertakings were largely household enterprises, the skills, knowledge, and attitudes handed down from parent to child. This was the case whether the household engaged in utilitarian or luxury production. The *Codex Mendoza* (Berdan and Anawalt, 1992, vol. 3: folios 57r, 70r) depicts male infants being handed at birth symbols of their future occupations: carpentry, feather working, codex painting, and gold working. It also depicts fathers teaching their sons the skills of working with wood, fine stones, feathers, gold, and painted codices (Figure 19). Girls were taught the spinning and weaving of cloth, along with other household skills, by their mothers. The number of people engaged in each of these crafts (and other occupations) was therefore limited by the number of offspring and other relatives in a household or by their ability to acquire apprentices or other skilled persons from neighboring households.

Some other specialized occupations were learned in schools, especially the temple-attached *calmecac*. There, noble boys were exposed to esoteric knowledge (as well as martial training) that prepared them to become teachers, scribes, bureaucratic officials, and priests. *Pochteca* were trained in merchant

Figure 19 A father teaches the lapidary craft to his son. Berdan and Anawalt (1992, vol. 4: folio 70r).

households and the merchant neighborhood collectivity (see Section 5). Still other occupations, such as midwifery, curing, divining, and medicine may have been mastered by an as yet undocumented system of apprenticeship.

Intensity refers to whether the specialization is a full-time or part-time activity. Elizabeth Brumfiel (1987) has suggested that full-time craft specialists plied their trades in cities, while part-time specialists were more commonly found in rural areas; the former focused primarily on the production of luxury goods, while the latter emphasized utilitarian goods. More specifically, Sanders et al. (1979: 180–181) and Parsons et al. (1982: 384) place luxury production in urban settings, especially Tenochtitlan–Tlatelolco. This urban–rural dichotomy seems to stem at least in part from a focus on luxury artisans (and others such as tribute overseers, scribes, and priests) as attached to palaces or temples. There were, however, many palaces beyond Tenochtitlan–Tlatelolco and the Basin of Mexico and many producers of luxury goods that worked as independent specialists.

The full-time/part-time distinction is a bit tricky when we move from generalizations to actual behaviors. For instance, a farmer whose agricultural schedule provides much free time in the winter months can (and did) devote those months to a convenient craft such as making baskets, sandals, obsidian blades, or colorful dyes and paints. During that time, it is entirely possible that the householders engaged in those activities full-time. And then, in the summer, they were full-time farmers. Is this, then, full-time or part-time work? To my mind, better understandings are achieved by incorporating "intermittent crafting" into the narrative on intensity (Hirth, 2009a; see Section 2). This furthermore allows us to view crafting, "in varying degrees of intensity at any point in a household's history, as a dynamic and risk-reducing component of diversified household economies" (Berdan, 2014: 104).

Economic interdependence was built into specialized systems since all people required a wide range of products, goods, and services, and few (if any) produced for their own needs or perceived needs. Some specialized persons were positioned as links in commodity chains, creating more profound economic dependencies (Millhauser and Overholtzer, 2020). These and other factors fed into complex and dynamic systems of distribution in Aztec heartland and periphery.

5 Forms of Distribution and Commercialization

Several factors and circumstances contributed to the need for goods and services to move from producers to consumers at the right times and places: ecological diversity, seasonality, crop failures, surplus production, specialization, little or no household self-sufficiency, high demand at key social and ceremonial moments, and wars.

In the Aztec world, forms of economic distribution were multifaceted and interconnected. Products, materials, and partially or fully finished goods moved through long-standing and well-understood channels. Some of these, such as gift-giving, were relatively informal and responded to both predictable and unpredictable situations and needs. Ceremonial occasions (from the birth of a child to a state extravaganza) required individuals and collectivities to acquire and distribute specific resources at specific times.

Other distribution channels reflected the intense commercialization of the Aztec economy: People obtained goods in marketplaces and through interactions with professional merchants who traded on local, regional, imperial, and international levels. Merchants were pivotal actors in moving goods locally and throughout the imperial domain and beyond, marketplaces were bustling and popular venues for exchanging virtually everything, supply and demand forces were at work, and commodity monies such as cacao beans and cotton cloaks facilitated exchanges.

5.1 Gifts and Offerings

Gift-giving was deeply embedded in and across all levels of Aztec society, from the most humble farmer to the haughtiest merchant to the most exalted ruler. Gifts and costly feasts cemented social affiliations and reinforced hierarchies. They confirmed and solidified symmetrical and asymmetrical political relations. And they fortified connections and communications between mortals and gods. Material goods were indispensable ingredients in all these relations as they moved about in obligatory giving and receiving (Mauss, 1990: 3, 13).

Any change in status or position needed to be acknowledged with feasting and gifts. Household rites of passage typically entailed feasting, an expense shouldered by the hosts. Relatives were feasted when greeting a newborn baby and celebrating its naming ceremony, during eagerly anticipated marriage ceremonies, and during less eagerly anticipated funerals. Parents dedicated their children to a school, later requesting their son's release from that school so he can marry – all with appropriate feasting, gifts, and scripted formalities (Sahagún, 1950–82, book 6: 127–128, 209). A typical wedding banquet would include flowers, ground cacao, tobacco tubes, and tamales (prepared over a span of two to three days) served in sauce bowls, ceramic cups, and baskets, much of which was purchased for the event (Sahagún, 1950–82, book 6: 129). While all households were expected to host such events, the quantity and quality of the food and drink supplied by the hosts were commensurate with the family's ability to pay.

Gifts were expected, indeed required, at these same life-cycle events ... but supplied by guests. As with feasting, gifts reflected the affluence of the giver. When greeting a newborn, for instance, rulers and nobles gifted large and precious capes or tunics, a less wealthy person presented a more run-of-the-mill cloak or loincloth or tunic, and a poorer person brought food and *pulque* (but apparently not clothing) (Sahagún, 1950–82, book 6: 196). Female wedding guests brought maguey fiber cloaks, small cloaks, or grains of maize to the ceremony, placing them before the hearth (one envisions a nice pile of gifts accumulating as the guests file in). Perhaps muting potentially stressful relations, mothers-in-law gave their new sons- and daughters-in-law gifts of clothing, which were then put on the bride and groom and tied together in the wedding's most emblematic moment (Sahagún, 1950–82, book 6: 129–131). While these gifting events appear one-way, it is clear that reciprocal gifting was expected in the long run.

Funerals likewise required gift-giving, since materials and goods were bestowed on deceased persons to assist them in their journey through the underworld. As in other life-cycle events, there were stark differences between poor commoners and wealthy nobles. Deceased commoners were wrapped in cloth and buried with bowls of maize, beans, chia, and other foods to aid them in their underworld journey (Chávez Balderas, 2007: 96–97). Wealthy merchants were sent on their way with their trade goods, which could include jaguar pelts, greenstone beads, copper bells, gold, and precious feathers (Figure 20; Boone, 1983: folio 68r). Rulers enjoyed the most extravagant send-offs, as they were given opulent gifts from other rulers who commanded great wealth. In 1502, the deceased Mexica ruler Ahuitzotl, for example, received slaves, precious stones, fine jewelry, gorgeous feathers, and cloaks from his allied and subject rulers to aid him in the afterlife. All this grand gift-giving was open and on display, a reflection of the status of both giver and recipient. Beyond wealthy and powerful rulers, others also contributed to Ahuitzotl's funeral, according to their means: "Poor widows and relatives could offer only a little food and clay or stone beads of the cheapest kind" (Durán, 1994: 383). Ahuitzotl was known as an especially generous ruler, and gift-giving from even the poorest commoners at this time reinforced this ruler's connections to his people and assured his legacy.

Gifts often accompanied explicit political messages. Some reinforced friendly (but always fragile) alliances. Some underscored political recognition such as the naming and seating of a new ruler (Durán, 1994: 298, 402–408). Some highlighted conflict, as when enemies invited to state extravaganzas arrived under cover and were given weapons and other martial objects, all to remind the visitors that "war and enmity existed between them" (Durán, 1994: 323). Still others signaled asymmetrical and opportunistic alliances, as between the empire and its client states (Berdan et al., 1996). In some cases, such as

Figure 20 Deceased merchant with his worldly goods. Nuttall (1903, folio 68r).

Axayacatl's consecration of a sacred stone monolith, Ahuitzotl's coronation, and Ahuitzotl's dedication of an expansion of Tenochtitlan's Great Temple, opulent gifts were presented from royal guests to royal hosts in customary greeting while hosts awed guests with even more exquisite gifts (Durán, 1994: 283–290, 319–327, 328–343). Each side presented exotic and expensive material objects to impress the other; even more to the point, the Mexica host Ahuitzotl used the flamboyant Great Temple dedication "to show Aztec grandeur and power to the enemies and guests and foreign people and fill them with bewilderment and fear" (Durán, 1994: 336).

There is a fine line between gifts and offerings. When material goods are presented in an explicitly religious context, they are often described as offerings. While this may imply one-way prestations, the Aztec faithful clearly expected reciprocity from the gods. An offering of small children to Tlaloc came with the expectation of rain; a ruler's gifts of luxury goods to the gods prior to battle carried the anticipation of victory; and farmers offered food, incense, *pulque*, and scripted speeches to their agricultural tools to assure successful harvests (Durán, 1994: 475; Durán 1971: 431–432).

The presentation and exchange of gifts and offerings were essential components of religious ceremonies, whether private or public. Most of the eighteen monthly ceremonies included household and/or *calpolli* feasting and mutual gifting (Sahagún, 1950–82, book 2). In addition to exchanging foods and other goods among themselves, people also made obligatory offerings of flowers and prepared foods to priests during many of those same ceremonies; in one variation, priests received gifts (or offerings) in exchange for incensing household objects (Berdan, 2007: 258). Offerings were sometimes made by specific residential or occupational groups, and some individuals and groups offered gifts of food, slaves, incense, and dances in fulfillment of sacred vows (Berdan, 2007, 2017).

All of this represents a continual behavioral and moral commitment to the act of giving, with people expending much time, energy, and physical resources. In addition to the direct costs involved, people also incurred opportunity costs, "the loss of gains from other productive activities in favor of ritual participation." Apparently, "perceived benefits from ceremonial involvement must have offset these direct and indirect economic costs" (Berdan, 2017: 151).

Goods circulated constantly through gift exchanges, offerings, and related means. There are innumerable additional examples, some of them more institutional, others more idiosyncratic. A ruler publicly and ceremonially presented special cloaks and military regalia to his valiant warriors; these gifts or rewards were inalienable and could not be transferred to any other person. During the devastating famine of One Rabbit (1454), Motecuhzoma Ilhuicamina emptied his warehouses to feed his desperate population, exemplifying the morality of gifting (although there was some self-interest, as he was trying to keep them from leaving). High-achieving individuals (including hunters) were granted awards during specific ceremonies. Debts were incurred. People gambled. Thieves were more or less successful. Judges accepted bribes (and were severely punished if caught). Huge amounts of materials and goods were collected and deposited in ritual caches, notably those in Tenochtitlan's sacred precinct (López Luján, 2005). Whatever the occasion or situation, bonds were mediated and secured through exchanges of goods and materials.

Once used, gifted and offered goods experienced different fates. Some, such as personal adornments and feathered regalia, could be reused in future rituals or on the battlefield. Clothing was usually worn until it wore out. Other goods dropped out of circulation: Food and drink were consumed by participants and priests, incense was burned, slaves were sacrificed, and flowers wilted. All manner of goods were interred or burned with the deceased or buried in ritual caches and not seen again until uncovered by modern archaeologists. All of this required frequent replenishment of materials and goods. These high levels of demand were met through the activities of tireless merchants and convenient access to the many marketplaces throughout the Aztec realm.

5.2 Marketplace Exchange and Money

Market exchange, broadly conceived, encompasses "the balanced exchange or purchase of goods where the forces of supply and demand are visible between two or more interacting parties"; they are reciprocal in nature where "value and price are determined through active negotiation" (Hirth, 2016: 60). Such transactions were found widely in ancient societies and could, theoretically, take place almost anywhere within a society. In the Aztec world, the most prominent venues for market exchanges were the numerous marketplaces (*tianquiztli*) found throughout the realm.

Two decades ago, I described marketplaces as "the lifeblood of the economic exchange system in Postclassic Mesoamerica" (Berdan, 2003: 94). I still hold to those words. Marketplaces stood out as hubs of economic exchange in the Aztecs' highly commercialized world. They also provided the equivalent of the modern newspaper or social media, circulating breaking news about social and political events of interest from word of a cousin's new baby to rumors of an impending war.

Much of what we know about native marketplaces derives from Spanish and colonial-era sources. *Conquistadores* toured the grand Tlatelolco marketplace prior to the conquest and provided detailed descriptions (albeit through their Spanish cultural lens). *Tianquiztli* persisted in their essential form after the conquest, when Spanish and Nahuatl descriptions abound. We can project these descriptions into pre-Spanish times with good confidence, accounting for additions such as wheat, chickens, iron tools, and Spanish *tomines* (Berdan and Smith, 2021: 190; Gibson, 1964: 352–353).

5.2.1 Marketplace Functions and Characteristics

Marketplaces served several economic functions in the Aztec world. They provisioned households with daily, periodic, situational, and extraordinary needs. They allowed households to expand and diversify their own economic production by providing outlets for their efforts. Marketplaces spaced throughout the landscape eased economic distribution by reducing transport costs where all goods were carried either on human backs or in canoes (Hirth, 2016: 80–82). In addition, marketplaces were sensitive to predictable cycles of variable demand, making available, for instance, an abundance of turkeys and dogs on feast days.

Wherever found in the imperial domain, marketplaces shared a common set of characteristics. They took place in centralized, accessible city-state locales, usually open plazas that were located adjacent to or near primary temples and palaces. These plazas were normally swept clean after market day (serving other purposes on nonmarket days), although the grand marketplace at Tlatelolco reportedly met daily and was surrounded with permanent arcades. All marketplaces convened on regular schedules, usually daily or at five-, thirteen-, or twenty-day intervals. Knowing these schedules, local people and more wide-ranging traders and consumers could convene in numbers sufficient to make economic exchanges worthwhile. Hernando Cortés, visiting the preconquest Tlatelolco marketplace, writes that 60,000 people assembled there daily; the Anonymous Conqueror accompanying him arrived at 20,000–25,000 people daily and 40,000–50,000 buyers and sellers at the larger five-day markets (Anonymous Conqueror, 1963: 178–179; Cortés, 1928: 87). Unfortunately, we do not know how they arrived at these figures. But even allowing for exaggeration, it is safe to say that this was a crowded, bustling, and noisy affair. Since buyers and sellers returned day after day, year after year, it must also have been economically viable and socially rewarding.

There was an understood and accepted order in the marketplace. Similar goods were sold in the same area of the venue, facilitating supply and demand knowledge among buyers and sellers (Figure 21). There were judges, at least in the largest marketplaces, and constables who circulated to deter or discover false measures, thefts, or any other trading misadventure. And there was a tax, although it is not entirely clear how it was assessed or to whom it was given, although it was most likely the city-state's ruler (for an in-depth discussion of marketplace taxes, see Hirth, 2016: 75–79). The marketplace was populated with people from all walks of life: Anyone with something to exchange could sell their goods or services in the marketplace. These ranged from individual householders with small lots of, say, chilis or eggs or cloth, to prostitutes plying

Figure 21 Copal resin in the modern Tepoztlan marketplace. Photograph by author.

their trade, to retailers traveling from marketplace to marketplace buying and selling commodities such as salt and cotton, to haughty professional merchants arriving from an exotic distant land with precious stones and shimmering feathers.

While all marketplaces exhibited the same set of essential characteristics and operated according to shared rules and valuations, they were not all the same. Some catered to large heterogeneous populations, others served smaller and more homogeneous settlements. One (Tlatelolco) sat at the hub of imperial power, others were located in city-states throughout the domain, and still others perched at the edge of empire. Some drew the attention of the imperial rulers; others were nearly invisible to it. Some were more successful than others in attracting traveling merchants. Some specialized in certain products and goods. They met on different schedules, and all responded to local ecological conditions and the changing fortunes of the expanding empire (Berdan, 1985, 2014).

The metropolitan marketplace at Tlatelolco was in a class by itself. Along with Texcoco, it was the only marketplace in the Basin of Mexico that met daily. Part of Tlatelolco's great success can be attributed to its accessibility – it could be approached by foot along causeways and by canoe across the lake. In addition, it served a concentrated, culturally diverse, and occupationally specialized population – not just Tenochtitlan and Tlatelolco but also surrounding city-states. This marketplace attracted sellers and buyers from all walks of life, purveying and perusing virtually everything from near and far.

Other marketplaces in the Basin of Mexico were widely recognized as "the place to go" for particular commodities: dogs at Acolman; turkeys at Tepeapulco and Otompan; slaves at Azcapotzalco; and ceramics, fine gourds, and cloth at Texcoco. One source (Durán, 1971: 277–278) states that specialized marketplaces were established by political order, although "specialization did not mean monopoly" as dogs, slaves, and other goods were sold in many other marketplaces, and all known specialized marketplaces also offered a wide range of other commodities (Berdan, 2014: 117–118). Still, Blanton (1996: 79) suggests that Basin of Mexico specialized marketplaces were established in relatively unimportant city-states by imperial conquerors, thereby depriving more powerful city-states of a marketplace's commercial benefits.

Marketplaces throughout the empire provisioned local populations, provided outlets for the wares of regional merchants, and sometimes served as entrepreneurial way stations for long-distance merchants. The majority of traders in these marketplaces were small-scale producers of their own goods, whether from their agricultural plots, kitchen gardens, or household crafts. Local production frequently coincided with nearby available resources; for instance, abundant clay sources facilitated pottery production, which in turn was reflected in a strong pottery area in the local marketplace. Provincial marketplaces also attracted

regional merchants, who often carried high-demand commodities across ecological zones, notably cotton, salt, and cacao. Professional long-distance merchants traded in a wide range of goods appealing to nobles and commoners alike,
but they were best known for trade in expensive commodities such as slaves,
decorated clothing, fine stones, and brilliant feathers (Durán, 1994: 258).

Some marketplaces commanded special attention from the imperial rulers.
For example, Tepeacac, situated close to Tlaxcallan, drew inordinate attention
from the empire. When conquered, Tepeacac was ordered to hold its market on
a specific day when a wide array of luxuries (such as gold, colorful feathers, rich
clothing, and jaguar pelts) must be available (Durán, 1994: 159). Whether
intended or not, this order may have encouraged people to trade at Tepeacac
instead of nearby Tlaxcallan (Hirth, 2016: 89) and assured that all professional
merchants had ready access to luxury wares. Beyond the imperial borders lay
international trade centers, "cosmopolitan trade venues at accessible locales,
where merchants from broad areas of Mesoamerica carrying a wide array of
exotic and expensive goods could interact" (Gasco and Berdan, 2003: 116).
These included well-known centers such as Cholula and Xicalanco, which were
perceived as more or less neutral and which attracted Basin of Mexico (and
other) entrepreneurs with their precious and ordinary goods and their royal
diplomatic assignments (Figure 22).

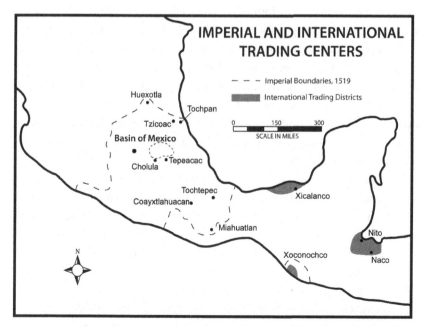

Figure 22 Major trading centers. Drawing by Jennifer Berdan Lozano.

Mutually agreeable prices were reached through bargaining or haggling, a practice common in Mexican marketplaces today. This practice allowed valuations to fluctuate daily or seasonally depending on available supplies, consumer demand, and individual preferences or circumstances. For instance, a pottery vendor was (and is) likely to settle for a lower price late in the day to avoid having to tote his or her weighty wares home. A potential purchaser knew this, and bargaining proceeded accordingly.

5.2.2 Money

Bargaining established not only the price but also the terms of exchange – barter or money (or, possibly, a combination of both). Barter, the exchange of goods/services for goods/services, was the most common means of sealing marketplace sales (for instance, a few large tomatoes for some dyestuff, or a turkey egg for some strips of pine bark). It apparently worked for all kinds of goods, even the most expensive: The Dominican friar Diego Durán (1971: 138, 286) informs us that merchants bartered "cloth for jewels, jewels for feathers, feathers for stones, and stones for slaves" and that "slaves were exchanged for cloths, which were called *cuachtli* [*quachtli*], jewels of gold and stones, and rich feathers."

Beyond barter, several forms of money facilitated exchanges in marketplaces throughout the commercialized Aztec world. Generally speaking, money is considered to perform four major functions: medium of exchange, standard of value, storage of wealth, and to enable payment (Neale, 1976: 7). For objects to qualify as money, they must be "widely accepted as measures against which other goods (or services) can be calculated" and perform mediation functions in actual exchanges (Berdan, 2014: 124). Cacao beans, large white cotton cloaks (*quachtli*), and copper axes stand out as media of exchange and standards of value in the Aztec world (Figure 23). Copper bells, stone beads, red shells, salt, and quills filled with gold dust are mentioned less often as forms of money.

Most of these goods were also useful commodities. Cacao was a widely enjoyed elite beverage, its value as a drink perhaps outweighing its importance as a medium of exchange (Millon, 1955). *Quachtli* cloaks may have served as male attire or utilitarian textiles, although that is not firmly documented. Copper axes ranged from fragile paper-thin objects (sometimes found as packets in caches) to rather heftier versions that could have been used as chopping tools (Hosler, 2003). Copper bells served as aristocratic gifts, bedecked godly idols, and accompanied the deceased on their journeys to the underworld; they were reportedly valued according to their size. Stone beads and red shells were

Figure 23 Cacao pod with beans. Photograph by author.

widely popular as articles of adornment, ritual offerings, funerary accompaniments, high-level gifts, and even gambling stakes (Durán, 1971: plates 32, 34; Durán, 1994: plates 49, 58; López Luján, 2005; Sahagún, 1993). All of these objects were paid in tribute to the Aztec empire. It is difficult to find a practical use for quills with gold dust; we have only the one observation by the conquistador Bernal Díaz del Castillo that measures of value (whether of cloaks, chocolate, slaves, or anything else) were determined by the length and thickness of the quills. Overall, the use of all of these as forms of money is understandable: They were durable, quantifiable, divisible, portable, and easily recognized (Berdan, 2014: 125).

Objects most commonly used as media of exchange were cacao beans and *quachtli* cloaks. Early colonial sources frequently mention the use of cacao beans as money. They point out that cacao could be exchanged for anything, whether purchasing commodities in the marketplaces, as payment for labor, or to pay fines (Berdan, 2014: 125, 304). Although these are colonial records, these uses of cacao beans were not a Spanish custom and it is likely that this represents continuity from pre-Spanish times.

The people of Aztec-period Mexico recognized several different types of cacao. Some were identified by their place of production, including Tochtepec, Anahuac (Gulf and Pacific coasts), and present-day Guatemala. Different varieties of cacao beans were paid in tribute to the Aztec empire, including "red cacao" from the Pacific coastal province of Cihuatlan. There is the possibility, offered by Francisco Clavijero (1970, vol. 1: 68), that the Aztecs used three species of cacao for money and one species for the drink (a small version called *tlalcacahuatl*). Clavijero claims that the species used for currency produced less palatable beverages.

Even though cacao beans could be likened to "small change," they were sufficiently valuable to draw the attention and considerable efforts of counterfeiters who removed or drilled through the bean's outer husk, extracted the chocolate, and replaced it with ground avocado pits, sand, or other such material. To disguise this deceit, the adulterated beans were mixed in with genuine ones to be sold to unsuspecting customers. Reportedly, the counterfeiters were so expert at their deception that it was almost impossible to detect the fake beans. To keep things in perspective, other vendors also might be less than honest: "the 'bad' bean seller mixed spoiled and infested beans with the good ones; the 'bad' maize seller arranged good grains atop fetid and mouse-gnawed ones; the 'bad' turkey seller offered old, sick birds" (Berdan and Smith, 2021: 185).

Large white cotton cloaks are also frequently mentioned as serving money functions. Higher in value, the cloaks complemented cacao beans in economic exchanges (one *quachtli* was worth 65–100 cacao beans). The cloaks were used widely: Slaves could be purchased (forty cloaks for a slave who could dance well and thirty for one who could not), "bathed slaves" were ransomed with *quachtli* on special occasions, and *quachtli* could be used as recompense for theft. They served as a standard of value for a wide range of commodities, at least in a 1554 document recording pre-Spanish tribute (Scholes and Adams, 1957). A person's standard of living was measured in terms of *quachtli*, whereby it was considered that an individual (perhaps a commoner) could support himself (and probably his family) for approximately one year on twenty *quachtli* (Motolinía, 1971: 367). These types of cloaks definitely circulated in the marketplaces. In one example, a young bride was given five *quachtli* by her new husband to take to the marketplace and purchase household provisions such as firewood, chilis, and salt. This is interesting in that such a large monetary "denomination" was used for small-value items. The young bride may have returned home with a handful of cacao beans in change, to spend on her next trip to the marketplace. At a more elite level, the ruler Ahuitzotl gave the professional merchants of Tenochtitlan and Tlatelolco 1,600 *quachtli* to exchange in the Tlatelolco marketplace for an unspecified number of fancy textiles, which the merchants traded in distant lands (Sahagún, 1950–82, book 9: 7–8; see Section 5.3.2). In both of these examples, *quachtli* were exchanged in marketplaces, in one case for household provisions, in the other to foster high-level trade and diplomatic relations in faraway regions. *Quachtli* were specifically listed as tribute items from twelve imperial provinces, to a possible total of 48,000 items annually (*Matrícula de Tributos*, 1980). It is likely that Ahuitzotl delved into these stores for his abovementioned trading venture.

In the to-and-fro of bargaining, there may have been some arguing about the value of the money forms themselves, since cacao, *quachtli*, and copper axes were not fully standardized as we expect in monies today. That is, the actual condition or quality of the money object came into play in determining its exchange value. There were different values for full or shrunken cacao beans (200 to 230), high-grade or low-grade cloaks, and pristine or worn copper axes – it was as if today a shiny new 50 pence coin were worth 60 pence while a dull, worn one would be worth only 40 pence (and how would it be determined how shiny or how dull the coin is?).

If cacao beans served as "small change," the cloaks were a larger denomination and were generally used for more expensive purchases. Similar to cacao, different grades of *quachtli* carried different values. Sahagún's Nahua associates tell us that different grades of cloaks were equal to 65, 80, or 100 cacao beans (Sahagún 1950–82, book 9: 48). These different values reflected the quality of cotton or weave ("fineness"), along with size. In an actual situation, buyer and seller would have to agree on the value of both cloak and commodity for a sale to take place. Bargaining must have required some mental gymnastics.

The condition of copper axes figured into their value. In 1548, copper axe monies were valued at four pieces equal to five Spanish *reales*. Their value diminished as they became worn, and when their value dropped to ten axes to one *real*, they were melted down. Reportedly they circulated widely in marketplaces in Guerrero and Oaxaca in pre-Spanish and early colonial times (Hosler, 2003: 168).

5.2.3 Market Integration

To the everyday bean seller or person out to replace a broken pot, the marketplace was convenient, useful, pleasurable, and necessary. But in a broader sense, it was more than that. In the first place, the Aztec world was highly commercialized, with marketplaces serving as magnets for complex systems of local and long-distance trade. Marketplaces were woven together into regional market systems that were "a regional network of interconnected marketplaces, including the market hinterlands they provision" occurring on a "regional, interregional, even a global scale" (Garraty, 2010: 10). In the Basin of Mexico, such a system appears hierarchical, as suggested by Blanton (1996). It consisted of two highest-rank marketplaces (the daily markets at Tlatelolco and Texcoco), five subregional centers that met on five-day schedules, five other subregional centers just to the north of the Basin, and several secondary centers. A similar hierarchy is suggested for city-states in neighboring Morelos (Smith, 2010). In this conceptualization,

marketplace exchanges were animated by high urban demand, local produc-
tion specializations, and ecological diversity. For instance, turkeys featured at
Otompan and Tepeapulco were transported from there to the marketplace at
Tlatelolco, where demand was high (Torquemada, 1969, vol. 2: 559). Chalco
Atenco served as a feeder market to Mexico City (Tenochtitlan) in early
colonial times, sending its leftover goods from its Friday market to Mexico
City's Saturday market – very likely a reflection of pre-Spanish practices
(Gibson, 1964: 358). In this case, rotating schedules contributed to marketplace integration. While goods moved hierarchically in this arrangement, they
also moved horizontally from nearby marketplace to nearby marketplace or
across regions through the efforts of traveling merchants. Some goods, such as
pottery, may have moved within definable spheres (Minc, 2009). Markets
usually met on rotating five-day schedules and often complemented neighboring marketplaces, making trading convenient for the locals and profitable for
professional entrepreneurs. In the Basin of Mexico, and probably elsewhere in
the empire, marketplaces were typically spaced eight to twelve kilometers
apart, a manageable day trip on foot for buyers and sellers (Hirth, 2016: 86). In
the late twentieth century in the Sierra Norte de Puebla, it was not unusual for
market-goers to walk for three hours each way across hill and dale to attend
their weekly market.

Second, marketplaces interfaced with production. They provided outlets
for household surpluses of local products, frequently reflecting the local
ecology and proximity to specific resources. It was no accident that
Coyoacan's marketplace featured wood products (from nearby forests) or
that Ecatepec's marketplace provided "Indian necessities" – salt, fish, and
maguey produced locally (Blanton and Hodge, 1996). Nichols (1994: 185)
argues that "the craft specialists at Otumba [Otompan] had a 'commercial'
orientation as well as a local one," supplying neighboring communities and
the broader region with goods such as lapidary ornaments, cotton and
maguey textiles, and obsidian core-blades and bifaces "through the market
and tribute systems." The strategic locations of some settlements allowed
them to specialize in transshipment activities, especially communities situated where trade routes and lakeshore converged in the Basin of Mexico
(Blanton, 1996: 72, 75).

Marketplaces not only facilitated household provisioning and exchanges of
small household surpluses; they also played a significant role in elite-level
production. Many luxury artisans were sponsored (and perhaps even housed)
by city-state rulers and high-ranking nobles. Many of these artisans' raw
materials were supplied by the sponsors' tribute stores. But not all. The
Tenochtitlan palace feather workers, for instance, would obtain their precious

feathers from their *tlatoani*'s storerooms or *totocalli* ("bird house"). But there was more to feather working than just feathers, and other necessary tools and materials such as obsidian blades, adhesives, dyes, cotton and maguey twine, bowls, and baskets most likely entailed a trip to the marketplace.

And third, marketplaces intersected with political goals and institutions in several ways. The prestige and reputation of a city-state ruler was at least somewhat measured by the magnificence of his city. A robust and attractive marketplace was an essential centerpiece in that magnificence. And the greater the marketplace activity, the more taxes collected by (supposedly) the ruler, although this may not have been a significant source of *altepetl* income (Hirth, 2016: 79). It is possible, at least in the highly competitive Basin of Mexico, that marketplaces were separated from conquered centers of political power as an intentional imperial strategy (Blanton, 1996: 77–83). In another vein, an aggressive imperial ruler, eyeing a lucrative conquest, first sent his disguised merchants to his target's marketplace to appraise the local political climate. In other imperial actions, conquerors sometimes meddled in their subjects' marketplaces; for example, Tepaneca conquerors shifted an important slave marketplace from Cuauhtitlan to Azcapotzalco (Bierhorst, 1992: 91), and Aztec overlords ordered Tepeacac's marketplace to be particularly friendly to long-distance merchants (see Section 5.2.1).

Beyond these direct political intrusions, marketplaces also played a role in imperial tribute assessments. Reportedly a vanquished city-state paid tribute to its conquerors in products and goods that were locally available. Apparently this did not necessarily require local production, since many city-states paid tributes in goods not locally produced but that were available in other parts of the imperial domain and beyond. Examples abound. On a large scale, raw cotton and colorful feathers (lowland products) were incorporated into the tribute of virtually every highland province in the form of cotton clothing and feathered regalia. Highland peoples gained access to these raw materials in marketplaces and through the efforts of traveling merchants. More specifically, materials that did not originate in the provinces paying them in tribute included amber for Xoconochco and turquoise and greenstones for Tochpan (Berdan and Anawalt, 1992). Again, reliable marketplaces and merchants were essential for the tribute payers to fulfill their obligations. In these and other cases, the conquest of a city-state and provincial area potentially afforded the conquerors access to economic resources beyond their new subjects' borders. In general, imperial rulers took a special interest in marketplaces that were located along major commercial routes, that moved goods across provincial borders into the hands of tribute payers, and that provided convenient venues for professional merchants dealing in luxury, status-related goods.

5.3 Merchants

5.3.1 Types of Traders

Producer-sellers were the mainstay of central Mexican marketplaces. Most were householders with small surpluses from their agricultural harvests, kitchen gardens, foraging activities, or in-home crafts. We see many of these individuals in Sahagún's (1950–82: books 8 and 10) descriptions of the Tenochtitlan and Tlatelolco marketplaces, designated as *-chiuhqui* (maker) and/or *-namacac* (seller). The same individual, depending on the immediate situation, was both producer and seller. For instance, the mat maker was a *petlachiuhqui* in his role as fabricator and a *petlanamacac* when he sold those same mats in the marketplace. Same individual, multiple roles. These sales were aimed primarily at household provisioning – compensating for seasonal shortfalls and trading for goods not produced at home. As already mentioned, household self-sufficiency rarely if ever occurred, and marketplace trading allowed all households access to the full range of everyday goods. These household traders potentially sold to rich and poor alike, all who needed, for instance, mats for sleeping, pots for cooking, and maize for tortillas.

There were, in addition, those who purchased the production of others to resell at a profit. These individuals were called *tlanecuilo* and often gained economically by obtaining goods in one region and selling them in another. They provided an important economic service by moving goods some distances across ecological zones into marketplaces convenient for people in cities, towns, and villages throughout the realm. Kenneth Hirth (2016: 156–178) differentiates six categories of pre-Hispanic retailers (recognizing the possibility for more that went unrecorded): vendors of foods, staple goods, textiles and clothing, high-value wares, specialty goods, and commercial operators. Within these categories, the broad range of goods handled by retailers points to their primary role as purveyors of commodities. Some of these, such as maize, fruit, and fish dealers, sold many types (and regional variations) of these products, suggesting the span of their operations. *Tlanecuilo* may have acquired their trade goods in their travels through marketplaces or perhaps directly from individual producers. This latter strategy may be seen at Otompan where some households produced certain items (such as molds and other ceramics) to excess (Nichols 2013). They may have sold some of these objects themselves, but it is just as possible that they sold them to local or traveling retailers who then traded them at a profit. On the flip side, Nichols (2013: 72) suggests that *tlanecuilo* brought various bowls, chocolate drinking cups, serving plates, dishes, and grater bowls to Otompan from Tenochtitlan and its vicinity. These traders must have found people receptive to their ceramic commodities and may have enjoyed exchange advantages in the active marketplaces at Otompan and neighboring communities. In a general sense, *tlanecuilo* may be characterized as regional merchants who individually trafficked in a diversity of goods; who transported commodities of medium or modest value such as cotton, cacao, and salt; who often traveled considerable distances across ecological zones; and who did all of this with profit as their priority (Hirth, 2016).

5.3.2 The World of the Pochteca

Merchants called *pochteca* and *oztomeca* are recorded as residing in twelve Basin of Mexico cities: Tenochtitlan, Tlatelolco, Cuauhtitlan, Azcapotzalco, Huitzilopochco, Mixcoac, Xochimilco, Chalco, Coatlinchan, Huexotla, Texcoco, and Otompan (Sahagún, 1950–82, book 9: 48–49; Figure 24). The name *pochteca* derives from the Tlatelolcan *calpolli* of Pochtlan, whose long-distance merchants must have gained sufficient renown that their name came to define similar merchants from other cities. The term *oztomeca* often appears in tandem with *pochteca*.

Figure 24 Basin of Mexico *pochteca* cities. Drawing by Jennifer Berdan Lozano.

It may have been used more generally to refer to "traveling" or "vanguard" merchants and survived into colonial times. For example, we find *oztomeca* from various communities selling their wares in the Coyoacan marketplace in the mid-sixteenth century (Anderson et al., 1976: 138–149).

Pochteca and *oztomeca* are usually described as professional merchants who traveled long distances in large caravans, dealing in luxury goods. But like so much in Aztec life, this was complicated and nuanced. It appears that some merchants "did have land to support their families" (Hirth, 2017: 87). They operated both as private entrepreneurs and as agents of their city-state *tlatoque*. As private entrepreneurs they traveled from marketplace to marketplace within the empire, always with economic gain in mind and trading in both low- and high-value commodities, from obsidian blades and rabbit fur to golden necklaces and rock crystal earplugs. They sold goods for rich and poor but were prominent in the Tlatelolco marketplace as purveyors of elite wares such as colorful feathers, decorated clothing, gold and stone jewelry, and jaguar pelts.

Professional long-distance merchants maintained close relations with artisans in their resident communities. The *pochteca* and feather workers of Tlatelolco appear to have enjoyed a symbiotic relationship whereby the merchants provided the artisans with exotic feathers and the feather workers provided the merchants with lovely finished goods for marketplace trading (Hirth, 2016: 81–82). Otompan, which had a *pochteca* enclave, was home to numerous craft industries that benefited from the distribution functions provided by their merchant neighbors (Hirth, 2016: 194–197; Nichols, 2013). And merchants commissioned by royal and other noble patrons delivered their hard-won exotic raw materials to palaces and their attached artisans.

Some *pochteca* and *oztomeca* directly served rulers and their city-states. They occupied a large room in Nezahualcoyotl's Texcoco palace (Douglas, 2010: 84), and three additional towns in Texcoco territory had a *pochteca* presence: Otompan, Huexotla, and Coatlinchan. As for Tenochtitlan, Ahuitzotl reportedly gave 1,600 large white cloaks (*quachtli*) to Tenochtitlan and Tlatelolco *pochteca* who traded those cloaks in the Tlatelolco marketplace for fine, decorated clothing. This exchange undoubtedly lightened the overall tumpline load, and also provided the *pochteca* with status-linked goods for appropriate exchanges with distant rulers. In this case, the rulers of the southern Gulf Coast reciprocated with precious greenstones, turquoise mosaic shields, seashells, tortoise shell cups, jaguar skins, and a multitude of glorious feathers (Sahagún, 1950–82, book 9: 17–19). *Pochteca* from only five Basin of Mexico cities (Tenochtitlan and Tlatelolco, and three from Tepaneca cities) traveled to the coast and participated in this exchange; *pochteca* in the Texcoco domain may have enjoyed similar privileges elsewhere. For those merchants restricted to trading within the empire, the marketplace at Tepeacac offered a convenient venue for access to luxury goods (see Section 5.2.1).

Extra-empire dealings have all the markings of diplomatic ventures with *pochteca* as intermediaries. Nonetheless, the *pochteca* as quintessential entrepreneurs also carried their own merchandise for trade in these same outlying centers. These locales, previously designated "ports of trade" (Chapman, 1957) and now more accurately described as international trading centers (Gasco and Berdan, 2003), provided reasonably comfortable and attractive trading venues for merchants from widely diverse regions. Neutrality was not necessarily a precondition: Aztec warriors may have been stationed at Xicalanco although Mayan merchants frequented that center, Xoconochco was an imperial province and also an international trading center, and Cholula was a famous trading center with a volatile political history. Merchants traveled to all of these centers (and more) with some assurance of safety, access to distant exotic goods, and economic profit.

Professional merchants provided additional valuable services to their *tlatoque* and the empire. They opened up lengthy and treacherous trade routes. They moved goods from unconquered to conquered regions, feeding into the tribute system and allowing the empire access to goods beyond their conquest borders. Additionally, merchants called *nahualoztomeca* ("disguised merchants") served their rulers as spies in outlying areas, ferreting out information on economic opportunities and the local political climate. Their role as state agents was well known, and it is no surprise that they (and their *pochteca* colleagues) were often accosted and even killed on the road for their wealth and political connections and that the Aztec powers retaliated with military force.

Ordinarily, *pochteca* were humble in dress and demeanor despite their sometimes considerable wealth. No doubt they presented something of an anomaly to the ruling elite – on the one hand, they were commoners who provided the aristocracy with status symbols; on the other, they challenged a jealous nobility with their accumulated wealth. No wonder they "played it down" in public. Concentrated in specific *calpolli*, they lived under defined organizational principles and demands but also enjoyed special perquisites. A hierarchical ranking system placed principal merchants at the top, followed by vanguard merchants, disguised and spying merchants, slave dealers, and slave bathers. They ritually honored their patron deity Yacatecuhtli, and every merchant was required to perform inspiring collective rituals before, during, and after their perilous journey; some carried the goods of other merchants who could not travel. Rank was based on achievement, and an individual wishing to climb the merchant hierarchy must gain sufficient wealth to purchase one or more slaves, ritually display and bathe them, and offer them for sacrifice in a prominent public ceremony. This was expensive and not only indicated the aspiring merchant's gratitude and loyalty to his colleagues and profession but also demonstrated his commitment to the community-at-large and its spiritual well-being. As for perquisites, the most obvious ones went to the principal merchants who were enlisted as royal agents and marketplace judges – powerful and visible roles.

6 Economic Development

The Aztec empire was the culmination of a long history of civilizations in Mesoamerica. In their prolonged migration and final settlement in Tenochtitlan in 1325, the Mexica and their fellow travelers encountered well-established economic institutions and activities, including diversified and specialized production, local and long-distance trade, established trade routes, marketplaces, tribute assessments, and political control of land. These economic features increased in scale during Aztec times, in tandem with the most compelling demographic and political dynamics of the time: unprecedented population growth, increase in urbanization, amplification of elites and their sumptuary requirements, intensification of city-state competition, and expanded warfare and conquest. Importantly, there was an intensification and expansion of agriculture and an increase in agricultural specializations and landscape modifications (such as terraces and irrigation canals). In the big picture, the Aztec world experienced a high degree of interconnectedness, whether commercial, political, social, or symbolic (Hirth and Nichols, 2017; Smith and Berdan, 2003).

As the Mexica moved from dependent mercenaries (1325–1430) to imperial overlords (1430–1521), they tightened their grip on their own economic security. Island Tenochtitlan initially had little in the way of a hinterland, its residents bartering lacustrine products for essential building materials and subsistence goods. In essence, the Mexica began "life at the bottom," developing their economic base in these early years. As latecomers to the Basin of Mexico they faced a political environment clogged with competing and manipulating city-states, all vying for survival and supremacy. As mercenaries in service to powerful city-states, the Mexica began accumulating lands and the attendant labor and tribute attached to them (Durán, 1994: 81). They increased their control over land, labor, and goods as they entered their imperial period.

In one particularly impressive move, in 1473 they gained control of Tlatelolco along with the grandest marketplace in the land, a magnet for commercial activity in the Basin of Mexico and beyond. Increasing commercialization was a hallmark of Aztec times, and the empire's heartland was a beehive of commercial activity. These marketplaces supplied increasingly large and dense populations with staples and utilitarian goods for everyone and preciosities for an increasingly insatiable elite. Exquisite luxuries and other goods were also acquired by *pochteca* merchants who traded them in marketplaces and made them available directly to rulers and nobles as their agents. As the empire's boundaries expanded, *pochteca* traveled farther and farther afield to access international trading centers, extending their rulers' access to exotic goods.

Pochteca and *oztomeca* merchants became increasingly important economic actors in the imperial period, their success deriving from their cunning entrepreneurial strategies. They were cooperative, collaborative, and competitive. Their communal organization afforded them protections and the ability to trade on a large scale, carrying their colleagues' wares as well as their own in wide-ranging travels. Rulers' recognition of the merchants' economic importance allowed the *pochteca* to gain political favor and even political positions, at least as marketplace judges. The merchants were cognizant of these advantages and prospects and apparently were becoming increasingly competitive and ambitious. Their insistence on going about humbly suggests a growing tension with the hereditary nobility, some of whom were less wealthy than some *pochteca*.

Aztec economic control was part and parcel of Aztec political power. As the empire expanded, more and more resources flowed into Tenochtitlan and its allied cities. Tribute demands also diversified as imperial armies marched into distinctive ecological zones. Specifically, they moved more and more into lowland and coastal regions, gaining direct access to status-linked luxuries such as colorful feathers, greenstones, jaguar pelts, and cacao. This was a convenient progression, since elite populations were also on the uptick and increasingly required these sumptuary goods. The aristocracy used these luxuries for lavish feasting, splendid displays, and palatial/urban enhancements, all of which were translated into political messaging as demonstrations of power and intimidation. More material control underwrote grander political theater and a competitive edge on the volatile city-state stage.

These tribute trends reflected local ecologies, demographics, and politics. For instance, Aztec conquerors in some recorded cases emphasized textiles in their immediate postwar tribute demands. This makes sense, since the male population would have been disproportionately reduced in the wars, and cloth production was women's work (Smith and Berdan, 1996: 282, 286, 292). The empire may also have altered its assessments on specific provinces because of new conquests or rebellions. For instance, Tochpan's initial tribute included fine feathers, which do not appear on the later *Matrícula de Tributos* and *Codex Mendoza* lists (see Figure 13). It is possible that local and imperial consumption had depleted the bird population, which was at the northern habitat fringe for macaws and other exotic birds. Precious feathers were paid by other conquered provinces, which perhaps became better sources (Berdan, 2014: 167–168). Another local factor was politics: Not only did the empire win and lose wars and subjects; so too were provinces politically complex and dynamic in their own right (see Berdan et al., 1996). Such was the case with Tlapa in Guerrero. That province's tribute increased dramatically over time, perhaps somewhat due to the annexation of additional territories to the province, "leading to reassessments in the tribute load" (Gutiérrez, 2013: 161).

Tribute assessments also responded to changing imperial consumption needs, especially the increasing demand for elite sumptuary goods met by increasingly far-flung conquests. Additionally, imperial rulers found themselves in need of specific goods such as warrior regalia presented as rewards for enemy captures. Most tributary provinces delivered one or another style of these feathered costumes. These were inalienable goods that needed to be constantly replenished. Royal construction projects, ritual obligations (such as burning copal incense), burial offerings, and other activities also took many tribute goods out of circulation. It was therefore essential for the empire, once underway, to continue expanding its thrall and access to ever-more distant, diverse, and exotic resources.

It is often said that trade preceded tribute, but we have seen that tribute also stimulated trade, production, and specialization in conquered provinces. For instance, feathered warrior costumes were fabricated and worn in battle throughout Mesoamerica; tribute demands assured that feather working would continue in conquered provinces and that some of this military regalia would be directed to the imperial overlords. Luxury and utilitarian crafts not only were produced in the Aztec heartland and in urban settings but were widespread in peripheral and rural areas as well; imperial conquest and tribute levies encouraged and even required the continuation of these activities.

It is clear that food and material production systems, local and long-distance trade, marketing, tribute, and all other aspects of the Aztec economy were adaptable and flexible. As populations increased, households moved their agricultural activities into new areas and/or intensified production with landscape modifications. They also diversified and enhanced their production with multicrafting, a clever strategy tied to the economy's increasing commercialization. Examples of specific economic changes detected archaeologically include increases in salt making associated with technological innovations (Millhauser, 2020) and fluctuating relations among maize variability, agricultural strategies, and political dynamics (Morehart and Eisenberg, 2010).

Exchange systems were also flexible. Tributes were adjusted to meet local capabilities and imperial needs, and in one well-documented case, tribute "deals" were made with Basin of Mexico people agreeing to resettle in an outlying battle-devastated land (Durán, 1994: 344–348). Marketplace prices rose and fell with seasons and daily with strategic bargaining. People moved about the landscape in response to stresses at home and opportunities elsewhere; they traveled in large migrations, regional relocations, and small treks. Some movements were politically motivated while others were economically inspired, leading to "a situation of considerable freedom of choice in the movement of artisans (and the high-level merchants)"; the transfer of luxury artisans to the Texcocan and Tenochtitlan royal palaces are cases in point (Alva Ixtlilxochitl, 1965, vol. 1: 326–327; Blanton, 1996: 83). City-states gained and lost in their success at manufacturing and marketing, such as the notable increase over time in pottery produced in and exported from Tenochtitlan to its larger region (De Lucia and Overholtzer, 2014: 454; Garraty, 2013: 169; Nichols, 2013: 73). Increased commercialization opened up consumer choices for commoners as well as nobles; for example, excavated sites in Morelos reveal that "nearly everyone had access to some imported painted pottery" (Smith, 2008: 168). And in trading for economic gain, merchants at all levels were opportunistic and creative in their dealings. In a culture where emulation and adoption of "foreign" objects and styles were customary, merchants could take advantage of enthusiastic and ever-expanding consumer demand.

Economic and political development was not neatly continuous and linear. It experienced many dips, for instance the droughts, famines, and insect infestations that played havoc with the food supply (Berdan, 2014: 54–55). Yet, even during the most devastating famine of 1454, some people survived by selling themselves and their families to Gulf Coast peoples; although they wept bitterly at this humiliation, some nonetheless willingly remained in those lands. Politically, the Aztecs were not the only powerhouses in the land: Wars with Tarascans and Tlaxcallans were as often calamitous as they were successful, and rebellions of subject provinces appear to have become increasingly frequent, interfering with tribute deliveries and blocking established commercial arteries. But still, new routes were opened and new wars initiated. It is tempting to speculate on the trajectory of the empire and its economy had not the Spaniards arrived. It does appear that Aztec imperial growth was slowing but that the economy was as vigorous as ever, relying heavily on increasing commercialization. While we often look at high-level political institutions and actors, which may come and go, the persistence of individual households and the "everyday actions of ordinary people" in economic dynamics should not be underestimated (De Lucia and Overholtzer, 2014: 441).

7 Future Directions

It is obvious from the foregoing that much remains unclear and unknown about the ancient Aztec economy. Too often have I had to use the words "perhaps," "it is likely that," "it appears that," or "there is some question." But all is not lost. Researchers continue to formulate challenging and productive questions. Some of these questions will require new data, others can employ sophisticated techniques in new ways, yet others may encourage looking at existing information through a different lens, and still others would benefit from constructive interdisciplinary approaches.

Targeted data collection and analyses can fill some gaps in our knowledge. For instance, current archaeological research at Tenochtitlan's ceremonial precinct has yielded thousands upon thousands of materials and artifacts, with the potential for uncovering countless more. Here is a wealth of information for future studies of trade, tribute, resource modification, religious investment, and ritual consumption (to add to the great many studies of this site already published). In another vein, archaeological research in Aztec-period provincial areas has shed light on direct and indirect imperial impacts in conquered areas, such as a lowering of living standards or a reduction in production activities following conquest (e.g., De Lucia and Overholtzer, 2014; Smith and Heath-Smith, 1994). Were similar impacts felt in other regions? What kind of regional variation was encountered by the empire, and what did that mean for both the conquered and the conquerors? Viewed somewhat differently, what demands did palace and empire make on its domain's resources, and how did those decisions affect life in the heartland?

Both archaeology and ethnohistory are benefiting from a surge in sophisticated scientific techniques. For example, the sourcing of obsidian and ceramics enjoys a long history, although some argue that further refinements would be revealing (e.g., Minc, 2017). A recent study sourcing turquoise has led to a rethinking of long-assumed trade patterns involving those precious and important stones (Thibodeau et al., 2018). Analyses of chemical residues from likely marketplaces offer another, albeit complicated, line of inquiry (as marketplaces were customarily swept clean after market day and also used for other activities) (Stark and Garraty, 2010). Documentary studies have gone beyond content and context to analyses of the physical documents themselves – an important case in point is the groundbreaking work in *Mesoamerican Manuscripts* (Jansen et al., 2019) that identifies paints and pigments and by extension relationships among people and materials. These and other advances in techniques bode well for the future of Aztec studies.

Beyond these inroads, intriguing questions still nag. Can we better understand the dynamic relationship between agricultural intensification (especially *chinampas*) and the state in the Basin of Mexico? How does the production of utilitarian crafts compare/contrast with the production of luxury crafts (the discovery of even one feather-working workshop, for instance, still awaits)? What was the role of collectivities (such as *calpolli* and merchant groups) in land rights and use and more generally in economic growth (e.g., Morehart, 2017)? Were all agricultural landscapes managed in the same way (e.g., *chinampas* versus maguey production)? How did professional merchants (*pochteca*) juggle their roles as state agents and private entrepreneurs? What effect did increasing flows of luxury raw materials and elite goods have on the economy of the Basin of Mexico? We continue to grapple with questions of elite control versus commercialization of the economy (see Blanton, 1996; Nichols, 2013; Stark, 2007; Stark and Garraty, 2010) and the "symbiosis between craftsmen, merchants, and the political elite in the Basin of Mexico (and elsewhere) is a major part of the political dynamic . . . but is little explored" (Blanton, 1996: 83). And future research could continue to expand our understanding of continuity and change in the Indigenous economy under Spanish rule. These (and other) questions and issues, by and large, address relationships among aspects of the economy, and among the economy and other dimensions of Aztec life, questions most productively approached through collaborative and interdisciplinary research.

References

Alva Ixtlilxochitl, F. de. (1965). *Obras históricas*. Mexico City: Editorial Nacional.

Alvarado Tezozomoc, F. (1975). *Crónica Mexicana*. Mexico City: Editorial Porrúa.

Anderson, A. J. O., Berdan, F. F., and Lockhart, J. (1976). *Beyond the Codices*. Berkeley: University of California Press.

Anderson, A. J. O. and Schroeder, S., eds. and trans. (1997). *Codex Chimalpahin*, vol. 1. Norman: University of Oklahoma Press.

Anonymous Conqueror (1963). The Chronicle of the Anonymous Conqueror. In P. de Fuentes, ed., *The Conquistadors*. Norman: University of Oklahoma Press, pp. 165–181.

Berdan, F. F. (1985). Markets in the Economy of Aztec Mexico. In S. Plattner, ed., *Markets and Marketing*. Lanham, MD: University Press of America, pp. 339–367.

Berdan, F. F. (1992a). The Imperial Tribute Roll of the *Codex Mendoza*. In F. F. Berdan and P.R. Anawalt, eds., *The Codex Mendoza*, vol. 1. Berkeley: University of California Press, pp.55–79.

Berdan, F. F. (1992b). Appendix C. In F. F. Berdan and P. R. Anawalt, eds., *The Codex Mendoza*, vol. 1. Berkeley: University of California Press, pp.158–159.

Berdan, F. F. (1996). The Tributary Provinces. In F. F. Berdan, R. E. Blanton, E. H. Boone et al., eds., *Aztec Imperial Strategies*. Washington, DC: Dumbarton Oaks Research Library and Collection, pp. 115–135.

Berdan, F. F. (2003). The Economy of Postclassic Mesoamerica. In M. E. Smith and F. F. Berdan, eds., *The Postclassic Mesoamerican World*. Salt Lake City: University of Utah Press, pp. 93–95.

Berdan, F. F. (2007). Material Dimensions of Aztec Religion and Ritual. In E. C. Wells and K. L. Davis-Salazar, eds., *Mesoamerican Ritual Economy*. Boulder: University Press of Colorado, pp. 245–266.

Berdan, F. F. (2014). *Aztec Archaeology and Ethnohistory*. Cambridge: Cambridge University Press.

Berdan, F. F. (2017). The Economics of Mexica Religious Performance. In D. L. Nichols, F. F. Berdan, and M. E. Smith, eds., *Rethinking the Aztec Economy*. Tucson: University of Arizona Press, pp. 130–155.

Berdan, F. F. and Anawalt, P. R. (1992). *The Codex Mendoza*. 4 vols. Berkeley: University of California Press.

Berdan, F. F., Blanton, R. E., Boone, E. H. et al. (1996). *Aztec Imperial Strategies*. Washington, DC: Dumbarton Oaks Research Library and Collection.

Berdan, F. F., Hirth, K. G., Nichols, D. L., and Smith, M. E. (2017). Introduction: Aztec Economy and Empire through the Lens of Objects. In D. L. Nichols, F. F. Berdan, and M. E. Smith, eds., *Rethinking the Aztec Economy*. Tucson: University of Arizona Press, pp. 3–16.

Berdan, F. F. and Smith, M. E. (1996). Imperial Strategies and Core–Periphery Relations. In F. F. Berdan, R. E. Blanton, E. H. Boone et al., eds., *Aztec Imperial Strategies*. Washington, DC: Dumbarton Oaks Research Library and Collection, pp. 209–217.

Berdan, F. F. and Smith, M. E. (2021). *Everyday Life in the Aztec World*. Cambridge: Cambridge University Press.

Berres, T. E. (2000). Climatic Change and Lacustrine Resources at the Period of Initial Aztec Development. *Ancient Mesoamerica* 11(1), 27–38.

Bierhorst, J. (1992). *History and Mythology of the Aztecs: The Codex Chimalpopoca*. Tucson: University of Arizona Press.

Blanton, R. E. (1996). The Basin of Mexico Market System and the Growth of Empire. In F. F. Berdan, R. E. Blanton, E. H. Boone et al., eds., *Aztec Imperial Strategies*. Washington, DC: Dumbarton Oaks Research Library and Collection, pp. 47–84.

Blanton, R. E. and Hodge, M. G. (1996). Appendix 2: Data on Market Activities and Production Specializations of *Tlatoani* Centers. In F. F. Berdan, R. E. Blanton, E. H. Boone et al., eds., *Aztec Imperial Strategies*. Washington, DC: Dumbarton Oaks Research Library and Collection, pp. 243–246.

Boone, E. H. (1983). *The Codex Magliabechiano*. Berkeley: University of California Press.

Brumfiel, E. M. (1987). Consumption and Politics at Aztec Huexotla. *American Anthropologist* 89(3), 676–686.

Brumfiel, E. M. (1991). Weaving and Cooking: Women's Production in Aztec Mexico. In J. M. Gero and M. W. Conkey, eds., *Engendering Archaeology*. Oxford: Blackwell, pp. 224–251.

Brumfiel, E. M., Salcedo, T., and Schafer, D. K. (1994). The Lip Plugs of Xaltocan: Function and Meaning in Aztec Archaeology. In M. G. Hodge and M. E. Smith, eds., *Economies and Polities in the Aztec Realm*. Albany, NY: Institute for Mesoamerican Studies, pp. 113–131.

Calnek, E. (1972). Settlement Pattern and Chinampa Agriculture at Tenochtitlan. *American Antiquity* 37(1), 104–115.

Calnek, E. (1976). The Internal Structure of Tenochtitlan. In E. R. Wolf, ed., *The Valley of Mexico*. Albuquerque: University of New Mexico Press, pp. 287–302.

Chapman, A. (1957). Port of Trade Enclaves in Aztec and Maya Civilization. In K. Polanyi, C. Arensberg, and H. W. Pearson, eds., *Trade and Market in the Early Empires*. New York: Free Press.

Chávez Balderas, X. (2007). *Rituales funerarios en el Templo Mayor de Tenochtitlan*. Mexico City: Instituto Nacional de Antropología e Historia.

Chávez Balderas, X. (2020). Bioarchaeology at the Sacred Precinct of Tenochtitlan. In D. Kurella, M. Berger, and I. de Castro, eds., *Aztecs*. Stuttgart: Linden-Museum, pp. 267–271.

Clavijero, F. J. (1970). *Historia Antigua de Mexico*. Mexico City: Editora Nacional.

Cline, S. L. (1984). Land Tenure and Land Inheritance in Late Sixteenth-Century Culhuacan. In H. R. Harvey and H. J. Prem, eds., *Explorations in Ethnohistory*. Albuquerque: University of New Mexico Press, pp. 277–309.

Cline, S. L. (1986). *Colonial Culhuacan, 1580–1600*. Albuquerque: University of New Mexico Press.

Coe, S. D. (1994). *America's First Cuisines*. Austin: University of Texas Press.

Cortés, H. (1928). *Five Letters of Cortés to the Emperor*. New York: W. W. Norton.

Costin, C. L. (1991). Craft Specialization: Issues in Defining, Documenting, and Explaining the Organization of Production. In M. B. Schiffer, ed., *Archaeological Method and Theory*, vol. 3. Tucson: University of Arizona Press, pp. 1–56.

De Lucia, K. (2017). Households in the Aztec Empire. In D. A. Nichols and E. Rodríguez-Alegría, eds., *The Oxford Handbook of the Aztecs*. Oxford: Oxford University Press, pp. 247–260.

De Lucia, K. and Overholtzer, L. (2014). Everyday Action and the Rise and Decline of Ancient Polities: Household Strategy and Political Change in Postclassic Xaltocan, Mexico. *Ancient Mesoamerica* 25(2), 441–458.

Díaz del Castillo, B. (2008). *The History of the Conquest of New Spain*. Albuquerque: University of New Mexico Press.

Diehl, R. (2004). Tula and the Tolteca. In F. Solis, ed., *The Aztec Empire*. Mexico City: Instituto Nacional de Antropología e Historia (INAH) and Conaculta, pp. 124–127.

Douglas, E. (2010). *In the Palace of Nezahualcoyotl*. Austin: University of Texas Press.

Durán, D. (1971). *Book of the Gods and Rites and the Ancient Calendar*. Norman: University of Oklahoma Press.

Durán, D. (1994). *The History of the Indies of New Spain*. Norman: University of Oklahoma Press.

Evans, S. (1991). Architecture and Authority in an Aztec Village: Form and Function of the Tecpan. In H. R. Harvey, ed., *Land and Politics in the Valley of Mexico*. Albuquerque: University of New Mexico Press, pp. 63–92.

Evans, S. (2005). Men, Women, and Maguey: The Household Division of Labor among Aztec Farmers. In R. E. Blanton, ed., *Settlement, Subsistence, and*

Social Complexity. Los Angeles, CA: UCLA Cotsen Institute of Archaeology, pp. 198–228.

Evans, S. (2017). Aztec Palaces and Gardens, Intertwined Evolution. In D. A. Nichols and E. Rodríguez-Alegría, eds., *The Oxford Handbook of the Aztecs.* Oxford: Oxford University Press, pp. 229–245.

Filloy Nadal, L. and Moreno Guzmán, M. O. (2017). Precious Feathers and Fancy Fifteenth-Century Feathered Shields. In D. L. Nichols, F. F. Berdan, and M. E. Smith, eds., *Rethinking the Aztec Economy.* Tucson: University of Arizona Press, pp. 156–194.

Fuentes, P. (1963). *The Conquistadors.* Norman: University of Oklahoma Press.

Garraty, C. P. (2010). Investigating Market Exchange in Ancient Societies: A Theoretical Review. In C. P. Garraty and B. L. Stark, eds., *Archaeological Approaches to Market Exchange in Ancient Societies.* Boulder: University Press of Colorado, pp. 3–32.

Garraty, C. P. (2013). Market Development and Pottery Exchange under Aztec and Spanish Rule in Cerro Portezuelo. *Ancient Mesoamerica* 24(1), 151–176.

Garraty, C. P. and Stark, B. L. (2010). *Archaeological Approaches to Market Exchange in Ancient Societies.* Boulder: University Press of Colorado.

Gasco, Janine and Berdan, F. F. (2003). International Trade Centers. In M. E. Smith and F. F. Berdan, eds., *The Postclassic Mesoamerican World.* Salt Lake City: University of Utah Press, pp. 109–116.

Gibson, C. (1964). *The Aztecs under Spanish Rule.* Stanford, CA: Stanford University Press.

Gutiérrez, G. (2013). Negotiating Aztec Tributary Demands in the *Tribute Record of Tlapa.* In K. G. Hirth and J. Pillsbury, eds., *Merchants, Markets, and Exchange in the Pre-Columbian World.* Washington, DC: Dumbarton Oaks Research Library and Collection, pp. 141–167.

Harvey, H. R. (1984). Aspects of Land Tenure in Ancient Mexico. In H. R. Harvey and H. J. Prem, eds., *Explorations in Ethnohistory.* Albuquerque: University of New Mexico Press, pp. 83–102.

Harvey, H. R. (1991). The Oztoticpac Lands Map: A Reexamination. In H. R. Harvey, ed., *Land and Politics in the Valley of Mexico.* Albuquerque: University of New Mexico Press, pp. 163–185.

Hassig, R. (1985). *Trade, Tribute, and Transportation.* Norman: University of Oklahoma Press.

Hassig, R. (1988). *Aztec Warfare.* Norman: University of Oklahoma Press.

Hendon, J. A. (2006). Textile Production As Craft in Mesoamerica: Time, Labor, and Knowledge. *Journal of Social Archaeology* 6(3), 354–378.

Hicks, F. (1984). Rotational Labor and Urban Development in Prehispanic Tetzcoco. In H. R. Harvey and H. J. Prem, eds., *Explorations in Ethnohistory*. Albuquerque: University of New Mexico Press, pp. 147–174.

Hicks, F. (1986). Prehispanic Background of Colonial Political and Economic Organization in Central Mexico. In R. Spores, ed., *Supplement to the Handbook of Middle American Indians: Ethnohistory*. Austin: University of Texas Press, pp. 35–54.

Hirth, K. G. (2009a). Craft Production, Household Diversification and Domestic Economy in Prehispanic Mesoamerica. In K. G. Hirth, ed., *Housework*. Archaeological Publications No. 19. Washington, DC: American Anthropological Association, pp. 13–32.

Hirth, K. G. (2009b). Housework and Domestic Craft Production: An Introduction. In K. G. Hirth, ed., *Housework*. Archaeological Publications No. 19. Washington, DC: American Anthropological Association, pp. 1–12.

Hirth, K. G. (2009c). Craft Production in a Central Mexican Marketplace. *Ancient Mesoamerica* 20(1), 89–102.

Hirth, K. G. (2016). *The Aztec Economic World*. Cambridge: Cambridge University Press.

Hirth, K. G. (2017). The Sixteenth-Century Merchant Community of Santa Maria Acxotla, Puebla. In D. L. Nichols, F. F. Berdan, and M. E. Smith, eds., *Rethinking the Aztec Economy*. Tucson: University of Arizona Press, pp. 68–101.

Hirth, K. G., Carballo, D. M., and Arroyo, B., eds. (2020). *Teotihuacan: The World beyond the City*. Washington, DC: Dumbarton Oaks Research Library and Collection.

Hirth, K. G. and Nichols, D. L. (2017). The Structure of Aztec Commerce: Markets and Merchants. In D. L. Nichols and E. Rodríguez-Alegría, eds., *The Oxford Handbook of the Aztecs*. Oxford: Oxford University Press, pp. 281–298.

Hodge, M. G. (1991). Land and Lordship in the Valley of Mexico: The Politics of Aztec Provincial Administration. In H. R. Harvey, ed., *Land and Politics in the Valley of Mexico*. Albuquerque: University of New Mexico Press, pp. 113–139.

Hosler, D. (2003). Metal Production. In M. E. Smith and F. F. Berdan, eds., *The Postclassic Mesoamerican World*. Salt Lake City: University of Utah Press, pp. 159–171.

Jansen, M. E. R. G. N., Lladó-Buisán, V. M., and Snijders, L., eds. (2019). *Mesoamerican Manuscripts*. Leiden: Brill.

Johnson, B. (2018). *Pueblos within Pueblos: Tlaxilacalli Communities in Acolhuacan, Mexico, ca. 1272–1692*. Boulder: University Press of Colorado.

Kellogg, S. (1988). Households in Late Prehispanic and Early Colonial Mexico City: Their Structure and Its Implications for the Study of Historical Demography. *The Americas* 44(4), 483–494.

Kelly, I. and Palerm, A. (1952). *The Tajín Totonac.* Institute of Social Anthropology Publication No. 13. Washington, DC: Smithsonian Institution.

Lewis, O. (1951). *Life in a Mexican Village.* Urbana: University of Illinois Press.

Lockhart, J. (1992). *The Nahuas after the Conquest.* Stanford, CA: Stanford University Press.

López Austin, A. (1973). *Hombre-Dios: religión y política en el mundo Náhuatl.* Mexico City: Universidad Nacional Autónoma de Mexico.

López Austin, A. and López Luján, L. (2009). *Monte Sagrado-Templo Mayor.* Mexico City: Instituto Nacional de Antropología e Historia.

López Luján, L. (2005). *The Offerings of the Templo Mayor of Tenochtitlan.* Albuquerque: University of New Mexico Press.

López Luján, L. (2019). The Codex Mendoza and the Archaeology of Tenochtitlan. In M. E. R. G. N. Jansen, V. M. Lladó-Buisán, and L. Snijders, eds., *Mesoamerican Manuscripts.* Leiden: Brill, pp. 15–44.

López Luján, L. (2020). The Sacred Precinct of Tenochtitlan. In D. Kurella, M. Berger, and I. de Castro, eds., *Aztecs.* Stuttgart: Linden-Museum, pp. 173–181.

Luttwak, E. (1976). *The Grand Strategy of the Roman Empire.* Baltimore: Johns Hopkins University Press.

Manzanilla, L. (2006). La producción artesanal en Mesoamerica. *Arqueología Mexicana* 14(80), 28–35.

Matrícula de Tributos. (1980). *Matrícula de Tributos, Museo de Antropología, Mexico (Col. 35–52).* Graz: Akademische Druck-u. Verlagsanstalt.

Mauss, M. (1990). *The Gift.* Translated by W. D. Halls. New York: W. W. Norton.

McCafferty, S. D. and McCafferty, G. G. (2000). Textile Production in Postclassic Cholula, Mexico. *Ancient Mesoamerica* 11(1), 39–54.

McClung de Tapia, E. (2000). Prehispanic Agricultural Systems in the Basin of Mexico. In D. L. Lentz, ed., *Imperfect Balance.* New York: Columbia University Press.

Medina-Rosas, P., López Luján, L., and Zúñiga-Arellano, B. (2021). Corales para los dioses: ofrendas marinas en Tenochtitlan. *Arqueología Mexicana* 28 (169), 20–29.

Millhauser, J. K. (2020). Let's Get Fiscal: The Social Relations of Finance and Technological Change in Aztec and Colonial Mexico. *Journal of Anthropological Archaeology* 60, 101196.

Millhauser, J. K. and Overholtzer, L. (2020). Commodity Chains in Archaeological Research: Cotton Cloth in the Aztec Economy. *Journal of Archaeological Research* 28(2), 187–240.

Millhauser, J. K., Rodriguez-Alegría, E., and Glasock, M. D. (2011). Testing the Accuracy of Portable X-ray Fluorescence to Study Aztec and Colonial Obsidian Supply at Xaltocan, Mexico. *Journal of Archaeological Science* 38(11), 3141–3152.

Millon, R. (1955). *When Money Grew on Trees: A Study of Cacao in Ancient Mesoamerica*. Doctoral dissertation, Columbia University.

Minc, L. D. (2009). Style and Substance: Evidence for Regionalism within the Aztec Market System. *Latin American Antiquity* 20(2), 343–374.

Minc, L. D. (2017). Pottery and the Potter's Craft in the Aztec Heartland. In D. L. Nichols and E. Rodríguez-Alegría, eds., *The Oxford Handbook of the Aztecs*. Oxford: Oxford University Press, pp. 355–374.

Mohar Betancourt, L. M. (2013). Los productos tributados a Tenochtitlan. *Arqueología Mexicana*, 21(124), 56–63.

Monzón, A. (1949). *El Calpulli en la organización social de los tenochca*. 1st series, No. 14. Mexico City: Publicaciones del Instituto de Historia.

Morehart, C. T. (2017). Aztec Agricultural Strategies: Intensification, Landesque Capital, and the Sociopolitics of Production. In D. L. Nichols and E. Rodríguez-Alegría, eds., *The Oxford Handbook of the Aztecs*. Oxford: Oxford University Press, pp. 263–279.

Morehart, C. T. and Eisenberg, D. T. A. (2010). Prosperity, Power, and Change: Modeling Maize at Postclassic Xaltocan, Mexico. *Journal of Anthropological Archaeology* 29(1), 94–112.

Motolinía (or Fray Toribio de Benavente). (1971). *Memoriales o libro de las cosas de la Nueva España y de los naturales de ella*. Edited by E. O'Gorman. Mexico City: Universidad Nacional Autónoma de Mexico, Instituto de Investigaciones Históricas.

Neale, W. C. (1976). *Monies in Societies*. San Francisco, CA: Chandler and Sharp.

Neff, H., Glasock, M. D., Charlton, T. H., Charlton, C. O., and Nichols, D. L. (2000). Provenience Investigation of Ceramics and Obsidian from Otumba. *Ancient Mesoamerica* 11(2), 307–321.

Nichols, D. L. (1994). The Organization of Provincial Craft Production and the Aztec City-State of Otumba. In M. G. Hodge and M. E. Smith, eds., *Economies and Polities in the Aztec Realm*. Albany, NY: Institute for Mesoamerican Studies, pp. 175–193.

Nichols, D. L. (2013). Merchants and Merchandise: The Archaeology of Aztec Commerce at Otumba, Mexico. In K. G. Hirth and J. Pillsbury, eds., *Merchants,*

Markets, and Exchange in the Pre-Columbian World. Washington, DC: Dumbarton Oaks Research Library and Collection, pp. 49–83.

Nichols, D. L., McLaughlin, M. J., and Benton, M. (2000). Production Intensification and Regional Specialization: Maguey Fibers and Textiles in the Aztec City-State of Otumba. *Ancient Mesoamerica* 11(2), 267–291.

Nuttall, Z. (1903). *The Book of the Life of the Ancient Mexicans Containing an Account of their Rites and Superstitions.* Berkeley: University of California Press.

Parsons, J. R. (1991). Political Implications of Prehispanic Chinampa Agriculture in the Valley of Mexico. In H. R. Harvey, ed., *Land and Politics in the Valley of Mexico.* Albuquerque: University of New Mexico Press, pp. 17–41.

Parsons, J. R. (2001). *The Last Saltmakers of Nexquipayac, Mexico.* Ann Arbor: University of Michigan Museum of Anthropology.

Parsons, J. R., Brumfiel, E. M., Parsons, M. H., and Wilson, D. J. (1982). *Prehispanic Settlement Patterns in the Southern Valley of Mexico: The Chalco-Xochimilco Region.* No. 14. Ann Arbor: Memoirs of the Museum of Anthropology, University of Michigan.

Parsons, J. R. and Parsons, M. H. (1990). *Maguey Utilization in Highland Central Mexico.* Ann Arbor: University of Michigan Museum of Anthropology.

Pool, C. A. (2012). The Formation of Complex Societies in Mesoamerica. In D. L. Nichols and C. A. Pool, eds., *The Oxford Handbook of Mesoamerican Archaeology.* Oxford: Oxford University Press, pp. 169–187.

Rojas Rabiela, T. (2001). Agriculture. In D. Carrasco, ed., *The Oxford Encyclopedia of Mesoamerican Cultures.* Oxford: Oxford University Press, pp. 3–8.

Sahagún, B. de. (1950–82). *Florentine Codex: General History of the Things of New Spain.* 12 vols. Salt Lake City: University of Utah Press.

Sahagún, B. de. (1993). *Primeros Memoriales.* Norman: University of Oklahoma Press.

Sanders, W. T., Parsons, J. R., and Santley, R. S. (1979). *The Basin of Mexico: Ecological Processes in the Evolution of a Civilization.* New York: Academic Press.

Sandstrom, A. (1991). *Corn Is Our Blood.* Norman: University of Oklahoma Press.

Saville, M. H. (1920). *The Goldsmith's Art in Ancient Mexico.* New York: Museum of the American Indian, Heye Foundation.

Scholes, F. V. and Adams, E. B. (1957). Información sobre los tributos que los Indios pagaban a Moctezuma, año de 1554. Documentos para la Historia del Mexico Colonial, vol. 4. Mexico City.

Smith, M. E. (1994). Economies and Polities in Aztec-Period Morelos: Ethnohistoric Overview. In M. G. Hodge and M. E. Smith, eds., *Economies and Polities in the Aztec Realm*. Albany, NY: Institute for Mesoamerican Studies, pp. 313–348.

Smith, M. E. (2003). Economic Change in Morelos Households. In M. E. Smith and F. F. Berdan, eds., *The Postclassic Mesoamerican World*. Salt Lake City: University of Utah Press, pp. 249–258.

Smith, M. E. (2008). *Aztec City-State Capitals*. Gainesville: University Press of Florida.

Smith, M. E. (2010). Regional and Local Market Systems in Aztec-Period Morelos. In C. P. Garraty and B. L. Stark, eds., *Archaeological Approaches to Market Exchange in Ancient Societies*. Boulder: University Press of Colorado, pp. 161–182.

Smith, M. E. (2012). *The Aztecs*, 3rd ed., Oxford: Blackwell Publishers.

Smith, M. E. (2015). The Aztec Empire. In A. Monson and W. Scheidel, eds., *Fiscal Regimes and the Political Economy of Premodern States*. Cambridge: Cambridge University Press, pp. 71–114.

Smith, M. E. (2017). Cities in the Aztec Empire: Commerce, Imperialism, and Urbanization. In D. L. Nichols, F. F. Berdan, and M. E. Smith, eds., *Rethinking the Aztec Economy*. Tucson: University of Arizona Press, pp. 44–67.

Smith, M. E. and Berdan, F. F. (1996). Appendix 4: Province Descriptions. In F. F. Berdan, R. E. Blanton, E. H. Boone et al., eds., *Aztec Imperial Strategies*. Washington, DC: Dumbarton Oaks Research Library and Collection, pp. 265–293.

Smith, M. E. and Berdan, F. F., eds. (2003). *The Postclassic Mesoamerican World*. Salt Lake City: University of Utah Press.

Smith, M. E. and Heath-Smith, C. (1994). Rural Economy in Late Postclassic Morelos: An Archaeological Study. In M. G. Hodge and M. E. Smith, eds., *Economies and Polities in the Aztec Realm*. Albany, NY: Institute for Mesoamerican Studies, pp. 349–376.

Smith, M. E. and Hicks, F. (2017). Inequality and Social Class in Aztec Society. In D. L. Nichols and E. Rodríguez-Alegría, eds., *The Oxford Handbook of the Aztecs*. Oxford: Oxford University Press, pp. 423–436.

Stark, B. L. (2007). Diachronic Change in Crafts and Centers in South-Central Veracruz, Mexico. In I. Shimada, ed., *Craft Production in Complex Societies*. Salt Lake City: University of Utah Press, pp. 227–261.

Stark, B. L. (2017). Imperialism and Gulf Ceramic Emulation: Comparison with Teotihuacan. In D. L. Nichols, F. F. Berdan, and M. E. Smith, eds., *Rethinking the Aztec Economy*. Tucson: University of Arizona Press, pp. 248–277.

Stark, B. L. and Garraty, C. P. (2010). Detecting Marketplace Exchange in Archaeology: A Methodological Review. In C. P. Garraty and B. L. Stark, eds., *Archaeological Approaches to Market Exchange in Ancient Societies*. Boulder: University Press of Colorado, pp. 33–58.

Stark, B. L. and Ossa, A. (2010). Origins and Development of Mesoamerican Marketplaces: Evidence from South-Central Veracruz, Mexico. In C. P. Garraty and B. L. Stark, eds., *Archaeological Approaches to Market Exchange in Ancient Societies*. Boulder: University Press of Colorado, pp. 99–126.

Tapia, A. de. (1963). The Chronicle of Andrés de Tapia. In P. de Fuentes, ed., *The Conquistadors*. Norman: University of Oklahoma Press, pp.17–48.

Thibodeau, A. M., López Luján, L., Killick, D. J. et al. (2018). Was Aztec and Mixtec Turquoise Mined in the American Southwest? *Science Advances* eaas9370, 13 June.

Torquemada, J. de. (1969). *Monarquía Indiana*. 3 vols. Mexico City: Editorial Porrúa.

Wells, E. C. (2012). Crafting and Manufacturing in Mesoamerica. In D. L. Nichols and C. A. Pool, eds., *The Oxford Handbook of Mesoamerican Archaeology*. Oxford: Oxford University Press, pp. 588–598.

Acknowledgments

This Element would not have seen the light of day without the foresight and support of the trio of series editors, Kenneth Hirth, Emily Kate, and Timothy Earle. Ken was the lynchpin for the Element, and working with him, as always, has been immeasurably productive and pleasurable. Emily eased it through its editorial hurdles, for which I am immensely grateful. I greatly appreciate the support and flexibility of Beatrice Rehl, the publishing director at Cambridge University Press. My thanks also go to three anonymous reviewers who offered useful comments on the Element. I am especially grateful to my daughter, Jennifer Berdan Lozano, for executing the maps and diagram and for managing the illustrations. My husband Bob was and is supremely supportive and, as a linguist, consistently finds those pesky words that elude me.

Cambridge Elements ≡

Elements in Ancient and Pre-modern Economies

Kenneth Hirth
Pennsylvania State University

Ken Hirth's research focuses on the study of comparative ancient economy and the development of ranked and state-level societies in the Americas. He is interested in political economy and how forms of resource control lead to the development of structural inequalities. Topics of special interest include: exchange systems, craft production, settlement patterns, and preindustrial urbanism. Methodological interests include: lithic technology and use-wear, ceramics, and spatial analysis.

Timothy Earle
Northwestern University

Tim Earle is an economic anthropologist specializing in the archaeological studies of social inequality, leadership, and political economy in early chiefdoms and states. He has conducted field projects in Polynesia, Peru, Argentina, Denmark, and Hungary. Having studied the emergence of social complexity in three world regions, his work is comparative, searching for the causes of alternative pathways to centralized power.

Emily J. Kate
University of Vienna

Emily Kate is a bioarchaeologist with training in radiocarbon dating, isotopic studies, human osteology, and paleodemography. Having worked with projects from Latin America and Europe, her interests include the manner in which paleodietary trends can be used to assess shifts in social and political structure, the effect of migration on societies, and the refinement of regional chronologies through radiocarbon programs.

About the Series

Elements in Ancient and Premodern Economies are committed to critical scholarship on the comparative economies of traditional societies. The Elements either focus on case studies of well documented societies, providing information on domestic and institutional economies, or provide comparative analyses of topical issues related to economic function. Each Element adopts an innovative and interdisciplinary view of culture and economy, offering authoritative discussions of how societies survived and thrived throughout human history.

Cambridge Elements $\equiv$

Elements in Ancient and Pre-modern Economies

Elements in the Series

Ancient and Pre-modern Economies of the North American Pacific Northwest
Anna Marie Prentiss

The Aztec Economy
Frances F. Berdan

A full series listing is available at: www.cambridge.org/EAPE

Printed in the United States
by Baker & Taylor Publisher Services